Rendezvous with the Wild
The Boreal Forest

To the volunteers, lifeblood of conservation

A BOSTON MILLS PRESS BOOK

Copyright © 2004 James Raffan

Published by Boston Mills Press, 2004
132 Main Street, Erin, Ontario N0B 1T0
Tel: 519-833-2407 Fax: 519-833-2195
e-mail: books@bostonmillspress.com
www.bostonmillspress.com

In Canada:
Distributed by Firefly Books Ltd.
66 Leek Crescent
Richmond Hill, Ontario, Canada L4B 1H1

In the United States:
Distributed by Firefly Books (U.S.) Inc.
P.O. Box 1338, Ellicott Station
Buffalo, New York 14205

Library and Archives Canada Cataloguing in Publication

Rendezvous with the wild : the boreal forest / edited by James Raffan.

Includes bibliographical references.
ISBN 1-55046-422-1

1. Taigas—Canada. 2. Taiga ecology—Canada. 3. Rivers—Canada.
4. Natural history—Canada. I. Raffan, James

QH106.R45 2004   508.71   C2004-902869-3

Publisher Cataloging-in-Publication Data (U.S.)

Rendezvous with the wild : the Boreal Forest / edited by James Raffan.
[196] p. : col. photos., ;   cm.

Includes bibliographical references.
Summary: A collection of art, photography, essays, stories, anecdotes, songs,
poems, journal entries, memoirs on the Boreal Forest of Canada.

ISBN 1-55046-422-1

1. Taiga ecology — Canada — Miscellanea. 2. Taigas — Canada — Miscellanea.
I. Raffan, James. II. Title.

577.3/7/0971/02 dc22   QH106.R46 2004

The publisher acknowledges for their financial support of our publishing program, the Canada Council, the Ontario Arts Council
and the Government of Canada through the Book Publishing Industry Development Program (BPIDP).

ONTARIO ARTS COUNCIL
CONSEIL DES ARTS DE L'ONTARIO

Jacket design by Gillan Stead. Text design by Gillian Stead and James Raffan

Principal front and back jacket photos by Fritz Mueller. Author flap photo by Gail Simmons.

Printed in Canada by Friesens (FSC-certified SW-COC-1271)
The pages in this book are printed on FSC-certified Domtar Luna, gloss, 100lb. text, using vegetable based inks.
(20% certified virgin wood fiber, SW-COC-880). This is the first hardcover book printed in Canada to carry the FSC label.

FSC
20% minimum
© 1996 Forest Stewardship Council A.C.

Rendezvous with the Wild
The Boreal Forest

EDITED BY JAMES RAFFAN

The BOSTON MILLS PRESS

Rendez-vous Boréal

Déclaration d'appui pour la conservation de la forêt boréale du Canada

Le 3 septembre 2003

Nous, les Canadiennes et les Canadiens, sommes responsables du maintien de l'une des dernières forêts intactes de la planète et qui constitue l'une des principales sources d'eau potable, d'air pur et de biodiversité au monde. La forêt boréale du Canada couvre plus d'un milliard d'acres, ce qui représente plus de la moitié de la superficie du pays. Elle est également habitée par plus de 600 communautés Autochtones, qui en sont les gardiens historiques. Le bien-être de l'humanité est profondément lié à la santé de cette vaste région forestière.

Aujourd'hui, le Canada a une possibilité unique de planifier la conservation de la forêt boréale afin que les générations futures puissent apprécier sa splendeur et récolter les bénéfices naturels qu'elle nous accorde. En tant que participants du Rendez-vous boréal 2003 organisé par la Société pour la nature et les parcs du Canada (SNAP), en partenariat avec la fondation David Suzuki et l'Initiative boréale canadienne, nous, les Canadiennes et les Canadiens, affirmons notre prise en charge de la protection de ce vaste trésor naturel.

LA LISTE DES SIGNATAIRES INCLUT:

** Aîné William Commanda

* Peter Allen, conseiller et partisan du programme boréal de la SNAP

Tom Cochrane, membre du Canadian Music Hall of Fame

Tara Cullis, présidente de la Fondation David Suzuki

* Wade Davis, membre de la National Geographic Society auteur et photographe

* Brian Deines, artiste et illustrateur de livres pour enfants

* Marc Déry, auteur-compositeur

Ken Dryden, personnalité reconnue du milieu sportif, auteur et président des Toronto Maple Leafs

* Margie Gillis, chorégraphe et interprète solo de renommée internationale

Sarah Harmer, auteure-compositeur

* Tomson Highway, O.C., auteur et musicien Cri

* Cathy Jones, actrice, comédienne et auteure récipiendaire de prix

* Thomas King, auteur, personnalité de la radio populaire

Silken Laumann, médaillée olympique à la rame et motivatrice

Jose Mansilla-Miranda, artiste

* Rebecca Mason, canoéiste et artiste du paysage

* James Raffan, auteur de best-sellers sur la nature sauvage et orateur

* Candace Savage, historienne culturelle et auteur

* David Schindler, professeur de renommée mondial et environnementaliste

David Suzuki, scientifique de renom, environnementaliste et personnalité de la télévision

* Veronica Tennant, O.C., première ballerine, personnalité de la télévision, conférencière et écrivaine

Florent Vollant, chanteur et compositeur récipiendaire de prix

* Parrain du programme boréal de la Société pour la nature et les parcs du Canada (SNAP)

** Parrain honoraire du programme boréal de la Société pour la nature et les parcs du Canada (SNAP)

Boreal Rendezvous

Declaration of support for the conservation of Canada's boreal forest region

September 3, 2003

As Canadians, we are stewards of one of the last remaining wild forest regions left on Earth and of one of the world's most important sources of fresh water, clean air and biodiversity. Canada's boreal region covers more than one billion acres — more than half of our country's landscape. These forests are also home to more than 600 Aboriginal communities, the historic custodians of this land. The well-being of all humanity is deeply entwined with the ongoing health of these great forest lands.

Today, Canada has the unique opportunity to conserve the boreal forest region by reinventing the idea of custodian so that generations to come may rejoice in the splendour and the natural benefits the boreal forest bestows upon us.

As participants in the 2003 Boreal Rendezvous, organized by the Canadian Parks and Wilderness Society in partnership with the David Suzuki Foundation and the Canadian Boreal Initiative, we, as Canadians, affirm our role as global stewards in planning for the health of this vast natural treasure.

THE LIST OF SIGNEES INCLUDES

** Elder William Commanda

* Peter Allen, CPAWS boreal advisor and supporter

Tom Cochrane, member of the Canadian Music Hall of Fame

Tara Cullis, president of the David Suzuki Foundation

* Wade Davis, explorer-in-residence at the National Geographic Society, author and photographer

* Brian Deines, artist and illustrator of popular children's books

* Marc Déry, Québecois singer and songwriter

Ken Dryden, acclaimed sports personality, author and president of the Toronto Maple Leafs

* Margie Gillis, internationally acclaimed solo dance artist

Sarah Harmer, critically acclaimed musician and songwriter

* Tomson Highway, O.C., Cree playwright, author and musician

* Cathy Jones, award-winning actor, writer and comedian

* Thomas King, writer and popular CBC Radio personality

Silken Laumann, Olympic medallist in rowing, motivational speaker

Jose Mansilla-Miranda, artist

* Rebecca Mason, canoeist, landscape artist

* James Raffan, author, geographer and governor, Royal Canadian Geographical Society

* Candace Savage, author, cultural historian

* David Schindler, professor, internationally acclaimed scientist and ecologist

David Suzuki, award-winning scientist, environmentalist and broadcaster

* Veronica Tennant, O.C., prima ballerina, broadcaster, lecturer, writer and director

Florent Vollant, award-winning singer and songwriter

* Signifies Patron of Canadian Parks and Wilderness Society (CPAWS) Boreal Program
** Signifies Honorary Elder of Canadian Parks and Wilderness Society (CPAWS) Boreal Program

SOLUTIONS ARE IN OUR NATURE

James Raffan

Contents

Donald Standfield

Foreword

ANNE JANSSEN

National Boreal Coordinator CPAWS

The boreal forest is named after Boreas, the Greek god of the north wind, and it embraces our northern hemisphere much like the wind encircles the planet. It is a vast and magnificent visual landscape whose beauty is subtle and sometimes best captured through other senses. I know when I have arrived in the boreal by the smell of the earth — centuries-old sphagnum moss, rich humus, sweet lichen and rock. It is the same smell wherever I go in the North, be that Russia, Northern Europe, or Canada.

Eight years ago, I began to work for the protection of the world's boreal forests through the Taiga Rescue Network in Sweden. My office was in Jokkmokk, a twelve-hour train ride north of Stockholm. The view out my compartment window was what eventually brought me back to Canada: for hours on end the scene did not change. Thousands and thousands of trees but not one single forest. Most of the Scandinavian forest has been turned into a tree farm with single tree species growing perfectly straight in precisely determined rows...row after row. Roughly five percent of the original forest is left in these countries where the ecologists search with their magnifying glasses for species that are indicators of a healthy old growth forest: lichens and fungi. The more obvious signs of a healthy ecosystem, such as the wolves and lynx, are now a rare occurrence in these small remnants of nature.

Soon after arriving in Sweden, at a meeting to determine our campaign priorities, we spent several hours discussing a remaining forest "hot spot" in Norway that required protection. Towards the end of the day it occurred to someone to ask how large the forest area was that we were discussing. The answer was six hectares. The last pockets of hope in this part of the world are that small.

Compare this to Canada, where we have 530 million hectares of boreal forest that is, for the most part, intact. We have healthy woodland caribou, bear, wolf and lynx populations, a landscape with vast wetlands, clear lakes and spectacular rivers; an area that has more fresh water than anywhere else on Earth; a place that purifies our water, produces fresh air and moderates our climate. The boreal is essential to our well being, to the health of each and every one of us, and to a way of life for millions of Canadians, including many aboriginal people. This is a unique place on our planet that remains intact and healthy, something almost unfathomable in this day and age.

I returned to Canada almost four years ago and in 2001 started working for Canadian Parks and Wilderness Society's (CPAWS) national campaign to protect Canada's boreal forests. The ongoing challenge in this work is that, in spite of its

Donald Standfield

beauty and significance, Canadians know very little about the forest that covers more than half of our country and stretches all the way from Newfoundland to the Yukon. We know more about the Amazon forest of Brazil than the forest in our own backyard.

We cannot protect something that we cannot name, so we set about naming it, and from this the Boreal Rendezvous initiative emerged, a national project and celebration to raise Canadians' awareness of the boreal. CPAWS was joined by three likeminded organizations: the David Suzuki Foundation, the Canadian Boreal Initiative and Mountain Equipment Co-op. Together we pulled off, in the summer of 2003, a series of ten canoe trips and many more related events across the country.

Joining us on these trips were many distinguished Canadians, a number of whom have contributed to this book. We knew that unless we engaged more than the usual suspects (environmentalists and canoeheads), it wouldn't matter how many beautiful rivers we paddled down, we wouldn't be able to capture public attention. It was heartening that in spite of their busy lives, these Canadians joined in the work (and play) to raise awareness about the boreal forest.

CPAWS has a vision for Canada's boreal forest. It is a vision that turns the map on its head. Rather than the current state of affairs in which the landscape is entirely fragmented and dominated by cities, industrial development, roads and concrete, and in which parks and havens of peace are few and far between, we propose a different scenario. In place of "the islands of wilderness in a sea of development," we envision a "sea of wilderness with (small, sustainable and viable) islands of development." We think our vision can be realized.

Virtually every part of Canada is currently under a land-use planning or industrial licensing process. This means that we have the next three to five years to decide the fate of this great forest. Canada is one of the few countries — if not the only one — that has the opportunity as well as the means to do it right. We can become world leaders, not only in how we conserve the forest, but also in the way we do it: by engaging local communities and First Nations people, and by ensuring sustainable economic development. This is a perfect role for us: a responsible, nature-loving nation that takes pride in being a good global citizen.

Throughout the summer of 2003, we celebrated while we paddled, heard stories, told stories, took photographs, laughed, wrapped our canoes, swatted black flies and were struck deeply by the magnificence of this country and the boreal landscape in particular. The media came along for the ride: interviewing Justin Trudeau as he retraced the footsteps of his father along the Nahanni River thirty years later; photographing Cathy Jones on her first portage; filming Ken Dryden paddling on the Athabasca River; and bringing images of the forest back to Canadians around the country.

This book captures the great moments and the great people that made the Rendezvous a reality. It was a dream that James Raffan and all the contributors made possible. *Rendezvous with the Wild* is a creative and heartfelt response to some of the most beautiful, undeveloped and, in some cases, threatened parts of Canada, a legacy of a journey and celebration that we hope will inspire others to join in our efforts to protect the boreal forest.

Turtle petroform in Whiteshell Provincial Park, Manitoba. James Raffan

Invocation

ELDER WILLIAM COMMANDA

I offer a prayer for Mother Earth and for the healing of nations
The struggles in the world are rooted in the land
This is the territory of my ancestors
My people were the Mamuwinini, the Nomads
We had no borders in the past
We respected all of Mother Earth
We did not own her
Our territory is of the land
It is in the air
It is in the waters
We travelled across Turtle Island in our canoes
My ancestors welcomed Cartier to this land from their 100 canoes
The canoes were made by hand, not the tools of industrialization
And they carried us far
Then the air and waters and land were pure and could sustain us
Now, the air and waters and land are poisoned
And the birchbark tree no longer grows tall
So we can no longer make our canoes
People are dying of cancers
Our relationships are poisoned
It is urgent, the need for us to take better care of Mother Earth
We must remember our sacred responsibility to Mother Earth
Only then will our relations with each other heal
Only then will we become a circle of all nations and a culture of peace

Prayer from the launch of Boreal Rendezvous, June 2003

Illustration by Marta Scythes

Elder William Commanda

ROMOLA VASANTHA

Elder William Commanda's range of interests is so broad and deep as to be overwhelming, in that he could as easily be seen as a spokesperson for racial harmony in South Africa as an advocate for indigenous justice in North America. Invariably, however, his prayer is drawn from his profound respect for Mother Earth.

William Commanda's ancestors were the Mamuwinini, whose birchbark canoes took them across the vast expanses of Turtle Island following the rivers that connected them with other sacred council fires, guided there by pounding rapids, by water embracing rock in a torrential song of power. The Mamuwinini created a protective web of pathways over the North American continent. The elder's symbolic connection to this spiritual heritage of his peoples is reflected by his world-acclaimed, uniquely stenciled birchbark canoes.

Thus, when he was invited by the Canadian Parks and Wilderness Society to help forge better linkages with aboriginal communities throughout the boreal forest, Elder Commanda was moved by the sincerity of the effort and decided at that time to share the teachings of three Wampum Belts, the sacred documents of the indigenous peoples' Turtle Island. His commitment to serve as honorary elder for the Boreal Rendezvous touched work that is closest to his heart — that being the reclamation of a non-adversarial relationship with Mother Earth, respecting her profound complexity, integrity and the inherent logic of her energy of balance and harmony.

In passing on that teaching, he inspired many of us who work hard to protect the environment to seek a deeper relationship with Gaia. Always, when he speaks, when he prays, when he conducts smudges to bring people together in common cause, Elder Commanda reminds us with increasing urgency of an indigenous prophecy that warns:

Elder William Commanda at the launch of Boreal Rendezvous in June 2003.
Evan Ferrari / CPAWS

Only after the last tree has been cut down,

Only after the last river has been poisoned,

Only after the last fish has been caught,

Only then will you find that money cannot be eaten.

Linda Anne Baker

The Boreal Forest covers 5.2 million square kilometres, about half of Canada . . .

Linda Anne Baker

. . . that's one quarter of the world's remaining intact forests, over one tenth
of the Earth's northern land surface, with all of the plants, animals, insects and birds that it houses . . .

Linda Anne Baker

making the boreal the single largest land-based ecosystem in North America

"Instead of calculating the minimum amount of forest that can be left intact to accommodate development, we need to ask how much can we afford to take out of the system and still safeguard it as a source of abundant natural species, vegetation and fresh water." Cathy Wilkinson

Linda Anne Baker

"Virtually every part of the boreal is currently under land-use planning or industrial licensing processes. This means we have the next three to five years to decide the fate of this great forest." Anne Janssen

Linda Anne Baker

"Rivers are the highways which join us together and allow us to visit each other." John Ralston Saul

Dark Pines Under Water

GWENDOLYN MacEWEN

This land like a mirror turns you inward

And you become a forest in a furtive lake;

The dark pines of your mind reach downward,

You dream in the green of your time,

Your memory is a row of sinking pines.

Explorer, you tell yourself this is not what you came for

Although it is good here, and green;

You had meant to move with a kind of largeness,

You had planned a heavy grace, an anguished dream.

But the dark pines of your mind dip deeper

And you are sinking, sinking, sleeper

In an elementary world;

There is something down there and you want it told.

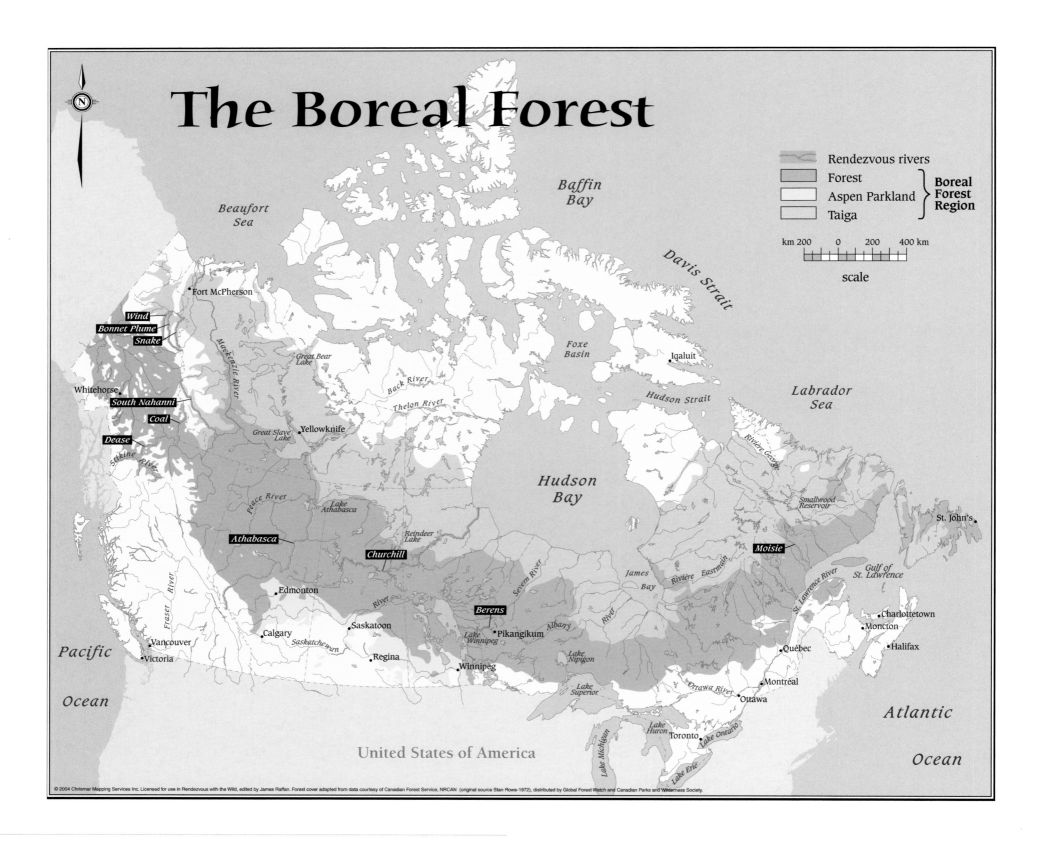

The Boreal Forest

Rendezvous rivers
Forest ⎱
Aspen Parkland ⎰ **Boreal Forest Region**
Taiga

km 200   0   200   400 km

scale

Beaufort Sea

Baffin Bay

Davis Strait

Foxe Basin

Labrador Sea

Fort McPherson

Wind
Bonnet Plume
Snake

Great Bear Lake

Back River

Thelon River

Hudson Strait

Iqaluit

Whitehorse

South Nahanni

Coal

Yellowknife

Great Slave Lake

Mackenzie River

Hudson Bay

Rivière George

Smallwood Reservoir

St. John's

Dease

Stikine River

Peace River

Lake Athabasca

Reindeer Lake

Athabasca

Churchill

Moisie

James Bay

Rivière Eastmain

Gulf of St. Lawrence

Fraser River

Edmonton

Berens

Severn River

St. Lawrence River

Charlottetown

Vancouver

Calgary

Saskatoon

Saskatchewan River

Lake Winnipeg

Pikangikum

Albany River

Lake Nipigon

Québec

Moncton

Halifax

Victoria

Regina

Winnipeg

Montréal

Pacific Ocean

Lake Superior

Ottawa River

Ottawa

Lake Michigan

Lake Huron

Toronto

Lake Ontario

Lake Erie

Atlantic Ocean

United States of America

Rendezvous with the Wild

The Journey Begins

JAMES RAFFAN

Like many Canadians, my home is snuggled up against the southernmost boundary of this nation, a comfortable refuge in the valley of the St. Lawrence River, from which I depart periodically by canoe or snowshoe to explore the upcountry wilds, the *pays d'en haut*, our national jungle, the boreal forest. So far — touch wood — I've always managed to skitter back to home and hearth to wash my socks and dream about ventures past and yet to come.

Along the way, I've met people who live and work in the boreal — First Nation folk and others from all walks of life — who know the woods in ways that a passing recreationist could never truly comprehend. When the forest feeds your family as well as your body and soul, there is a relationship that words or pictures could never describe. But because of the sheer size and scope of this forest that hangs on the shoulders of this nation like a great green scarf, peaceful coexistence between and amongst the various groups who would inhabit the boreal has been ensured largely by avoidance. The loggers go where the trappers and paddlers are not, and vice versa. Timber leases have been written, park boundaries negotiated, and protected areas delimited, often in more or less total isolation. There have been conflicts, but most of us have gone our separate merry ways, doing the things we do, and taking the boreal for granted.

It was the hope of the Canadian Parks and Wilderness Society (CPAWS), in conjunction with forward-thinking members of the forest industry, the conservation movement, and some of the six hundred First Nations communities inside the boreal forest, that Boreal Rendezvous would begin to change all that — change the way we think about the forest,

James Raffan

Valley of the Jacques Cartier River in March. James Raffan

bring people together in common purpose on a national scale, change the way we interact with each other in matters of development and conservation, and change the way we conduct any kind of human enterprise that touches or affects the boreal.

It was the slightly revolutionary nature of Anne Janssen's description of this ten-trip cross-Canada canoe extravaganza that initially caught my fancy two winters ago. CPAWS and its partners and affiliates hoped to raise general awareness about the value and significance of the boreal forest by bringing a diverse constellation of Canadians together on a series of river trips from one side of the boreal to the other. In doing so, CPAWS would celebrate the boreal and show by example how to work together, for the good of the people, for the good of the forest.

This book is a testament to the success of Boreal Rendezvous. Contained in these pages are the thoughts, journal notes, sketches, songs, photographs, artistic images and musings of more than seventy of the people who took part in Boreal Rendezvous. It is not so much a book

Editor James Raffan
Gail C. Simmons

about the forest — although it surely does illuminate some of Canada's boreal splendour — as it is a response to the wild and a look to the forest's future. It is geographically and seasonally spotty (I couldn't resist including an image of winter in the boreal, which is my absolute favourite time to dwell in the woods), but what it lacks in comprehensiveness I'm hoping it makes up for in the diversity and depth of feeling behind each contribution.

Here are the voices of artists and scientists, paddlers and elders, forest workers and conservationists, as well as contributions from many people who blur or defy traditional categories — scientists who are also artists, elders who are paddlers, forest workers who are staunch conservationists. Added to these, to round out the collection somewhat, are visual and verbal contributions from others who care deeply about the boreal.

The original idea for this book — which faded quickly when I saw the range of Boreal Rendezvous participants — was to assemble a dozen or so essays, each written by one of the participants from a different perspective, and to illustrate these with photographs of the boreal taken during the summer of 2003. However, with the creative input of John Denison, Noel Hudson and the editorial team at Boston Mills Press, the idea morphed into a less restrictive concept and design that would take better advantage of the expressive capabilities of Rendezvous participants and present a wider range of contributions that we hope will create a much more engaging experience for readers.

The challenge of the new idea was to find a thread with which to stitch together this richly diverse set of contributions. The packages that arrived — envelopes, paper boxes, cloth pouches, duct-taped containers, plastic bags, and every permutation of electronic dispatch (which at times totally befuddled my wood-powered Macintosh computer) — were as varied as the people who created them, and what they contained was even more interesting. In the end, because the premise is simple and accessible and grows naturally out of the essence of Boreal Rendezvous, I've chosen to organize the book as a journey, a journey by canoe through the boreal forest from west to east.

Entering the boreal. Red Lake bush pilot Hugh Carlson banks his prized Norseman toward the headwaters of the Berens River in northwestern Ontario.

James Raffan

The journey has four legs: we begin on rivers in the Yukon (Boreal Northwest), then move into British Columbia and Alberta (Western Boreal), on into Saskatchewan, Manitoba and Ontario (Central Boreal), and finally curve up into Québec and Labrador (Eastern Boreal). In this part of the book, "rendezvous" works best as a verb, meaning the act of assembling people en route to a previously appointed place. We invite readers to join with a remarkable group of writers, artists, guides, and compadres to travel across the country in words, images and songs.

The final destination in the book — where the term "rendezvous" works best as a noun, meaning meeting place — is the Ojibway village of Pikangikum on the Berens River, where a historic agreement was signed in the summer of 2003. Though small in geographic scope, the agreement is emblematic of the new way of doing business in the boreal that Anne Janssen talked about at the very early stages of the Boreal Rendezvous project. And the agreement is a fine place for us all to assemble and think about where to head next.

The virtue of Bill Mason's much loved, leaky, cumbersome campfire tent — the view. James Raffan

Boreal Rendezvous participants overlook the impressive Snake River valley. Fritz Mueller

LEG 1

Boreal Northwest

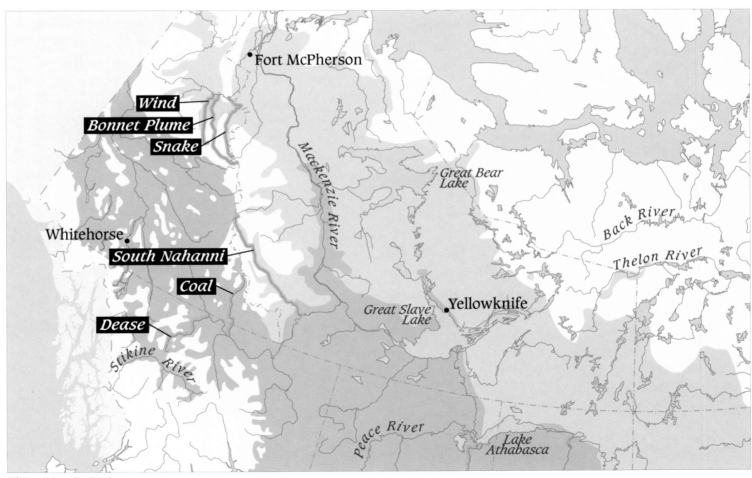

Chrismar Mapping Services

Our Sacred Generations
Our Rivers, Our Life, Our Future

ELAINE ALEXIE

I am from the Tetlit Gwich'in First Nation. I was raised along the shores of the Peel River in the central Yukon Territory. The very words *Tetlit Gwich'in* translate in my language as "The People of the Headwaters." They identify the connection that has bound my people to our northern homeland for centuries.

For countless generations, the Peel River watershed has provided us with rich sustenance in terms of wildlife, landscape and plants. Not only does this watershed provide for our physical needs, but it also continues to supply spiritual nourishment to our people.

Oral traditions and storytelling are strong in this area. There are many signs of sacred burial sites, stone axe cuttings and traditional trails to be found within the Peel watershed. These sites give evidence of the traditional lives of our ancestors.

For youth such as myself, major industrial plans paint a different picture of our future. Three major tributaries of the Peel River — the Wind, Snake and Bonnet Plume — are in serious threat of environmental degradation from proposed natural resource development. Large-scale hydroelectric dams, oil and gas exploration, iron ore mining, steel processing plants, and coal-bed methane strip mines are among the current plans of government and industrial groups within the Peel watershed.

Rivers nationwide, and watersheds such as that of the Peel River, are ecologically fragile. It is important to protect these areas for their biological diversity.

Young people of the Tetlit Gwich'in, as well as youth of the Nacho Nyak Dun Nations, our southern neighbours, must stay connected to our cultural and spiritual identity as indigenous peoples. We need to take a firm stand on what we feel our future should be, for ourselves, our descendants, and for the environment.

Our existence is being sacrificed to sustain the global need for energy. Most people do not perceive that the world is heavily influenced by their consumption, nor do they understand where their energy comes from.

Elaine Alexie speaking outside the Museum of Civilization in Ottawa at the conclusion of Boreal Rendezvous. Roberta Walker / CPAWS

It enables a society to grow, but from a northern perspective, the lives of the everyday people within these small communities tell a different tale about consumption.

Our lives are intertwined with the land. The land is sacred to us. Harvesting the land must always be done while keeping in mind its sustainability for the future. We must make formal practice the habit of ensuring that there is something left of the land for our children and for our grandchildren.

We may be in social and economic transition, but we all have the power to protect the last pristine environments of our country. Promotion of safe, alternative, renewable energy development that will not harm our environment must happen. We must look for alternatives to fossil fuels and educate ourselves on reducing consumption, for the sake of the land, but also because indigenous peoples are the ones most greatly affected by the short-term economic development policies created to satisfy the industrialized world's seemingly limitless desire for energy.

Just as life is derived from the land, in return we must respect its power and sacredness. Rivers such as those within the Peel watershed must continue to flow to provide for our environment and to ensure the well-being of families and communities for now and for generations to come. *Haih Kíeh* — Great Thanks.

Elaine Alexie's great-great-grandfather William Vittrekwa in his smokehouse at "Eight Mile," on the shores of the Peel River near Fort McPherson, NWT, in the summer of 1978. James Raffan

Balancing People and Place

JOHN RALSTON SAUL

On September 3rd, 2003, a few dozen canoeists, including myself, set off from Victoria Island on the Ottawa River to paddle a mere kilometre downstream to the Museum of Civilization. More precisely, we canoed from Aboriginal territory in the heart of the national capital to the site of an historic Aboriginal settlement. That site reminds us that Ottawa is not the nineteenth-century creation of ambitious politicians and lumber barons. It is the continuation of millennia of gathering people together there, where rivers meet; bringing people in from all directions.

In fact, the northern half of North America has never been about static, defended territories. It has always been about people moving along the rivers through the territory.

And it remains what it has always been, a land tied together by a mosaic of rivers and lakes. There is no real break between the aboriginal era, the three centuries of initial immigration with its settlement patterns, and today's postmodern nation state.

Today we may drive and fly in utilitarian manners, cutting across the physical reality of our country. But the country remains itself. It is its own truth, one defined by moving water.

If we pretend otherwise, we will end by destroying what makes the geography work — work for itself and so for us, its custodians. Of all the nation states in the world, this is the one where it is most obvious that an indifferent pseudo-rational imposition of short-term human demands leads straight to a deep physical breakdown. And from that moment on, the humans, along with everything else, will suffer.

Why? Despite the strength of the rivers and the power of the land, all of it depends on a fragile balance of marginal climates, thin soils and interwoven patterns of natural support. This is not a place like those of mid-Europe and mid-America. It is not a place of moderate climate and deep loam.

Perhaps the most convincing and fascinating detail that demonstrates this overwhelming strength and fragility is the canoe itself. John Jennings has pointed out that Canada is the only one of the vast territories around the world invested by the Europeans in which they simply accepted the local means of communication — the canoe. They had no choice. The place dictated the means of transport. Over the centuries the immigrants did little more than enlarge the canoe and change the material from which it was made. The full history of the opening up of Canada is the history of canoes on rivers and lakes.

John Ralston Saul (bow) with paddling partner Bob Jickling in heavy water on the Snake River during their trip in the summer of 2003. Lachlin McKinnon

A few decades ago, our small group paddling down the Ottawa River would have had to make its way through log booms, past pulp and paper mills. I remember those great booms from my childhood visits to Ottawa. Today the only reminder of that massive assault on the boreal forest is the great strength of the river's current that carried the logs out of the North.

After our group had landed beneath the Museum of Civilization, there was a small ceremony on the shore. As I sat there in that clear softening September sun, I couldn't help looking around at the astonishing place in which we almost unconsciously found ourselves. Once off the water you can look back and get a sense of the river pouring out of the North. This was the great highway to and from the interior. Champlain was led up these waters by Aboriginals for whom it was the established route, up to the Madawaska, along it, across Lake Nipissing and down the French River into Georgian Bay. And that is only a tiny fraction of the great highway, a miniscule fraction of the mosaic of moving waters into which the Aboriginal peoples introduced us and which became the Canadian mosaic. You have only to sit on the eastern bank of the Ottawa and stare across the flood of water to the Parliament buildings on the highest cliff opposite to understand that Canada, unlike almost any other country in the world, does not see rivers as frontiers or liquid walls that separate warring peoples and armies. Rivers are the highways that join us together and allow us to visit each other.

That the Parliament buildings were placed on the highest cliff is a double reminder — first of Ottawa as a millennial gathering place for people to meet and talk, but also the buildings were consciously placed there at a time when rivers were still the principle means of communication for everyone. From a great distance away the water travellers would see the palace of the people.

Finally, sitting on that shore you are overwhelmed by that great human construction. And yet the Parliament buildings are only marginally European. In fact, they hardly seem to be a construction. More profoundly they resemble a magical eruption from the ground, animist and irregular. And facing them from across and below is Douglas Cardinal's Museum of Civilization, built out of the land, not upon it — a rejection of rationalist structures. It is a constant reminder that we can live in this land and build the physical representations of our civilization without basing them upon European traditions. His building is a convincing demonstration of our ability to build a civilization that is part of the land and not a submission to it.

Storm Cloud Mountain
Marten Berkman

Hoy dia, el vuelo de un Aguila Real, quebro el ritmo de mi remar por el rio Snake. El Aguila Real poso majestuosa sobre la cabeza mitica de los spruces negros. ¡Vision de los Tiempos!

Today, the flight of a golden eagle broke the rhythm of my paddling on the Snake River. The golden eagle perched majestically on the mythic head of black spruces. Vision of the Time!

José Mansilla-Miranda

In the spring of 2003, CPAWS invited me to join one of their canoe trips down Canada's boreal forest rivers. It happened that six months earlier I had arranged to do just that with friends from Whitehorse.

I immediately agreed to become honorary patron of their ten-river series of trips through the very foundation of Canada's environment, but for myself, I canoed down the Snake River in the northern Yukon that summer on a personal trip — 300 kilometres from an altitude of 4,200 feet down to 300 feet at an alarming speed, around great boulders, avoiding cliff faces and passing through a remarkable land of beauty, along the edge of a mountain range I had not imagined existed, past grizzlies, caribou, mountain sheep, beneath peregrine falcons and eagles.

The Canadian cliché is that few of us have seen or will see this beauty. And that is true. But that is not entirely a fault or a weakness either of Canadians or of these places. They are far away. Their equilibrium is delicate. They cannot support the visit of many of us. And in any case, these are not touristic destinations in the classic sense. Their purpose is not to be gawked at by the curious or even to provide us with passing emotions. Their role is far more real, far more vast. We are speaking of a great deal more than beauty in its abstract or romantic sense.

These places, these boreal forests and rivers, are the land of which history has made Canadians — all of us — custodians. And those few of us who have seen these places have an obligation to speak of them; to describe to other Canadians their country, our country.

Much of river canoeing is about finding the line that will take you down the current. If you were able somehow to stand aside and watch yourself canoeing down these waters, you would see impossible turbulence, destructive counter currents, rocks concealed just beneath the flow, snags of upturned trees. That outside view — the view of structured society and human domination — might make you see a trip down the river as a competition; an opportunity for heroics. You against nature.

But, of course, it has nothing to do with competition and heroics. You do not win if you successfully make your way downstream. Rather you succeed because you blend yourself into the river. You find the line that carries you between the impossible turbulences, counter currents, roots and rocks — the natural timeline down the river, with the river, with the flow of nature. Often this line is made up of a series of eddy lines, with great speed on one side and static water on the other, a few lateral inches that make the difference between surging forward and taking refuge in the calm. The true line lies a few centimeters to one side or the other of that divide.

The eddy line becomes a metaphor for civilization — that is, for societies that live a long time precisely because they learn how to live with their place rather than brutishly attempting to defeat it.

My friend Bob Jickling, a wonderful canoeist who organized our trip, said that the first few days out, people tend to gawk at the beauty around them. Then gradually they begin to fit in, to find their own way down the line, to become part of the place. But not a static part and certainly not an intellectual part. It is all moving. It has its own truth. All you can hope to do is find your ephemeral place in this movement. That was exactly what happened.

I say this to make a simple point. We must move away from the old idea of opposites, the Manichean view of the world, black or white. We must stop opposing two impossible opposing visions of the North: a perfect, museum-like protection of the wilderness set against raw nineteenth-century commodity exploitation.

My point is not that we must seek a compromise between the two. That is the worst sort of working agreement — one in which two unworkable, human-centred obsessions are made to work with each other. After all, the idea of an empty place is a human — indeed urban and southern — view of nature as distant and occasionally a playground. As for the idea of exploitation, it is a very similar form of human delusion: that we can simply subject geography to our short-term needs.

Both positions deny the long-term ability of humans to live in and with nature — the possibility of which our Aboriginal history demonstrates. One excludes humans. The other gives humans every right and justifies long-term destruction by invoking the need for northern jobs. Both of these are the equivalent of gawking at nature.

We have another tradition upon which our civilization was built: that of guardianship. We must reinvent that idea of guardianship as the key to our long-term relationship with the land and its water.

In the South we take as our right a long-term view of education and careers and housing and stability. We have a middle-class view of long-term societal patterns.

In the North, the equivalent right would be guardianship. It contains the possibility of long-term jobs — the equivalent of stable middle-class jobs for northerners; jobs not necessarily based merely on the boom-and-bust cycles of old-fashioned exploitation.

Take the example of the Haida people of the west coast. They have negotiated the co-management with Parks Canada of a park called Gwaii Haanas. It is a new model which puts them at the centre with long-term, well-paid jobs as guardians. That is one model.

Of course some places must simply be protected. In many places, protection should not mean that the historic custodians lose their natural rights to live from the land. That may be part of its reality. And in others — where conditions are appropriate — there will be commodity exploitation.

Coloured pencil journal sketch, July 25, 2003.

Desde las montanas; un triangulo coronado de spruces exprimio sabia nueva, sobre la catedral vacia del cuerpo. ¡Pontifice/Lobo, estan abiertas las puertas de las estrellas! Hablo a la encarnaciones del alma, la boca del Tiempo.

From the mountains, a triangle crowned by spruces poured new sap on the empty cathedral of the body. Pontiff/Wolf, the star's doors are open! It talked to the incarnations of the soul, the Voice of Time.

José Mansilla-Miranda

Donald Standfield

In some places, such as the watershed of the Nahanni, it seems that, with the leadership of the Dene, most damaging mining will soon be prevented through the enlargement of the national park. This will also involve a management — guardianship — approach that will put the Deh Cho First Nations at the centre of what happens there. And yet, because we are unwilling to face the small costs of removing a few mines, we may leave a few sites intact, which could destroy all the good we have done.

All of this is about how all Canadians can exercise our custodianship in the North — largely through those who wish to live there and hope their children and grandchildren will live there — not in old-style boom-and-bust cycles, but with their place and thanks to a very long view of how they can live in the North without damaging it. They have seen how much of the old-style generation of wealth simply didn't stick, let alone multiply into long-term wealth. How many mines have come and gone? How many logging camps? Where is the long-term downstream wealth? It just washed through, leaving little behind.

How do we re-imagine that long-term custodianship? Perhaps we begin with northern education. Most of it is still designed on a southern model, so that the more educated you are the more likely you must leave. Or it offers training aimed at the boom-and-bust jobs. All of this is as if education in the North exists only to fuel a war between northern ways and schooling. Even the simple timings of school years and exams are designed in southern provinces to cut northerners off from their land. Exams are timed to coincide with hunting seasons in order to force kids into an artificial choice between the southern way and the northern way. This is the new, subtle racism: get educated or go out on the land. Surely going out on the land should be an integral part of northern education. That same education could be designed to develop a long-term commitment to place and to the realities of that place.

In other words, we all need to be supportive of re-imagining long-term stable life in the North. And that is tied to custodianship of the land.

These rivers and forests are far away from most of our lives. They are close to the lives of the Gwich'in and the Dene and other northerners, whether Aboriginal or not.

What they tell us — and what a trip down one of these rushing rivers of rocks and rapids and canyons and mountains, some mauve, some black, some striped red reinforces — is that the roots of our existence in our cities, the environmental roots as well as the mythological, lie in the North, in the boreal forests and rivers, and in the Arctic which lies beyond.

If Canada is to exist, we must be able to imagine the whole country; imagine something very unusual for a country which thinks of itself as industrialized but is also an enormous uncontrollable territory. We must move away from the simplistic idea of human domination over place and towards a balance between people and place; a balance that says we are a new kind of high civilization that can imagine itself living in and with this land for as long as the trees grow, the sun rises from the east and sets in the west, and the rivers flow.

Hollow hair from moulting caribou floats freely at crossing places and decorates the high-water marks on northern rivers. James Raffan

Calling All Caribou

BRIAN BRETT

Elder Jimmy Johnny
Fritz Mueller

For some time I've been thinking about wilderness. I don't know when this started, perhaps on the Wind River — on a high plateau lined with ragged, nameless peaks, on a clear aquamarine ribbon of light littered with a geological kaleidoscope of river stones.

During my twenties I burned out my knees on the mountains, hauling an eighty-pound Number 2 Trapper Nelson canvas-and-birch-frame packsack through some of the wildest regions of British Columbia. The wilderness was always "out there." A concept native to my European roots. It was a place where I went, separate from home.

I thought I knew wilderness, but it was only as I watched it disappear that I realized I never understood where I had been. Despite the rugged mountain journeys of my youth I had always been a tourist. I didn't live it, even when I spent months in lonely cabins or slept on spruce needles under a canvas tarp.

Gazing at the bright Wind River stones slipping by, it dawned on me that I was just "visiting" again, along with most of my fellow travellers. For many indigenous people, however, the wilderness is home, and I got a glimpse of this as we prepared for this trip.

The N'yak Dun elders prepared a little feast and ceremony for us in Mayo before we set off, and there I met one of the men who would travel with us, Jimmy Johnny, all snappy and sharp, wearing a cowboy shirt I instantly coveted.

A quiet, rugged man, Jimmy shot his first moose at age nine, was a wrangler at thirteen and a guide at sixteen. He only missed one out of the next forty-two years in the mountains. When it came time to leave, he had traded his flashy shirt for bush wear — an old flannel shirt over jeans with the knees out and cracked leather boots, topped off with a cowboy hat so ancient and moldy it appeared to be growing lichens. Though I teased him about his hat, I felt quietly embarrassed by my fancy new gear, and he made me feel nostalgic for the canvas days of my youth.

One day we were camped out on the high plateau of the Wind. A few of us, including Jimmy, decided to go for a walk across the tundra plain that was between us and the mountain where there was a good salt lick beside a lake.

We'd been walking about fifteen minutes when Jimmy stopped, and stared down the valley. "Caribou," he grunted, pointing at a distant speck on the tundra. He walked ahead of us. "Spread out," he told us.

Then, half crouched, he started stepping back and forth, sideways, putting his weight first on one foot and then the other, holding his fingers up on both sides of his cowboy hat, and wiggling them. He'd only performed this shuffling, slow dance for a few seconds when that caribou dot made a hard right turn and began advancing towards us.

For several minutes Jimmy lost himself in this slow, dignified ritual and we watched the caribou come charging up the valley, now crisscrossing, attempting to catch our scent, rearing, its muzzle high in the air, its enormous rack like a spider web against the sky.

It advanced the final fifty feet dancing on its hind legs, shaking its rack, muzzle flaring, until suddenly, not more than 150 feet away, it caught our scent, dropped to all four legs, and took off for the mountains while we smiled with wonder, watching it run.

"That's the way we hunted caribou in the old days," Jimmy said with a grin. And, at that moment, I felt that peculiar warmth you only feel so often in your life — the moment when you know you are standing next to someone grounded in his world. This is when I realized we were guests in Jimmy Johnny's home, and for him the real wilderness was "out there" — back in the city.

Adrift in a Sea of Caribou

JOYCE MAJISKI

The North seems like a barren place until you're suddenly surrounded by more grunting, snorting life than you can fathom.

She is large, four-legged and coming right for me. With big, dark eyes intent upon me, she draws nearer. I wonder how close she'll come. Another step. I can nearly reach out and touch her. Suddenly, with an explosive snort and a sideways leap, she throws up her head, scuttles backward, and clatters off.

Watching ten thousand caribou is a study in flow dynamics. As part of the herd moves in one direction, thousands race the other way for no apparent reason, the wild dashes making the mass of animals unpredictable. As I watch them roam up and down the valley far above us, my anticipation mounts. Will they drop down in our direction or simply disappear into another valley?

Then it happens. The herd heads toward us. The herd moves with surprising speed, and suddenly I am surrounded. Thousands of caribou surge around me, snorting and barking low coughs. Waves of swirling brown part and pour past me. Thousands of feet upon thousands of legs churn the soil, kicking up dust and sending hair airborne. The restless power of the herd is palpable. They are so close, yet even while sitting in the middle of it all, there is no fear. I am adrift in a sea of caribou.

We've travelled ten days through empty land. It seems impossible that there can be so many caribou in one place. Yet here they are. Timing, as they say, is everything. It takes four months for the herd to travel almost four hundred miles from wintering grounds in the northern Yukon to the calving grounds in northern Alaska. Each year they make the journey, and to come upon them like this, to be here, is a gift, rare and unexpected.

The caribou move almost gently over the land. Occasionally energy builds within the herd, sending ripples through the mass of animals until a group suddenly leaps across the river, calves floundering and cows bawling. I think about how all of this, the power and beauty, is threatened by oil development in the refuge. What will be the final cost?

I lose count of the numbers and am swept up in the details: the mottled and molting coats, the myriad shades of brown, the barnyard smell, the clicking of tendons, the graceful, sweeping antlers of the black-brown bulls — most still in velvet — that spring slightly as they run.

Large, dark eyes look down impossibly long noses, staring at me. I don't belong. I want to grow two extra limbs and join them.

Across the river, an island in the sea of movement appears. Calves, tawny and adorable, settle down beside watchful cows for a rest. Standing over their young, the mothers shuffle, snort, twitch, shake, and snort again. With the constant harassment from flies and mosquitoes, adult caribou are never completely at rest. Their incessant twitching and shaking makes even me fidget. It also loosens tiny puffs of caribou hair that float in the breeze, the same hair we'll see floating downriver for days.

Caribou Cresting,
2001 etching, 18" x 24,"
100-percent rag, French
printmaking paper.
Joyce Majiski

When rested, the calves stand, stretch and run for their mothers. The calf mortality rate will be about fifty percent, with half the deaths due to cows and calves becoming separated during river crossings and because of the confusion of such a large herd. One calf scratches its ear delicately, then some unseen signal is given and the migration begins again. For almost six hours, wave after wave of caribou crosses the river as the herd heads up behind us to the next valley. Eventually the flow of animals lessens, and only a few stragglers dot the valley.

After they have all passed, the fresh scars on the hillside are the only evidence that their passage was real, not a dream. For days before, we had seen the crisscrossed trails that grace the country, ancient migration paths worked by millions of caribou. We had questioned whether there could actually be that many caribou.

As we wander back to our tents, the land suddenly too quiet, we have our answer. Humbled and exhausted, we make coffee and marvel at our luck. If we had been up the valley even just a short distance, we would have missed the whole event. In the morning we'll move on. I wonder if it would be too much to ask to see them just one more time.

An earlier version of this essay appeared in the December 1999 issue of *Backpacker* magazine.

Writer Teresa Earle makes notes in her Wind River journal. Fritz Mueller

Snippets from a Wind River Journal TERESA EARLE

July 26 — Most of us are huddled around the campfire nursing cups of tea, being treated to an impromptu concert by Yukon recording artist Joe Bishop, one of our colourful guides. Two days ago we flew into McClusky Lake, a placid subalpine lake just large enough to land a single-engine Otter. Here we swam and basked in July's intense northern sun and brushed up on our strokes in preparation for the Wind River.

Our camp is on a gravel flood plain covered in mats of mountain avens gone to seed. Many in the group have already scaled the plush moss- and berry-covered ridge that overlooks the camp and report the possibility of blueberry picking. This campsite is surrounded on all sides by the high ridges and velvety green flanks of the Wernecke Mountains.

The Wind meanders and periodically braids, but is essentially a Class II flow of riffles, fast, tight turns and the odd powerful eddy. The feature that makes the most lasting impression is the extraordinary water — so clear and clean it sparkles with an icy blue-green hue. We skim across an illuminated river bottom, in and out of patches of warm sun, and watch Arctic grayling leaping from the eddies.

July 29 — Our coterie of artists, photographers, writers, community members and guides is becoming a tight-knit crew of river kin. We laugh lots, share wonderful stories and revel in this special river together. Our second layover was mostly grey and overcast, an exception on a journey that has seen the weather change almost hourly. Clouds stream by from the west, and we imagine that our Three Rivers companions on the Bonnet Plume and Snake are seeing similar patterns in the weather.

Berry picking has become a central activity. We indulge in berry sauce drizzled on cheesecake and French toast, berries in pancakes and granola, and berries by the fistful as we go walking through the verdant woods. Scoured, angular mountains provide endless opportunities for hikes and walks. Some evenings the sun streams in under the clouds and casts an orangy blush across the peaks, illuminating stark ridges and washing slopes in red, black, green and white.

The rainbow of rocks at our feet is as alluring as the scenery. We crouch over to examine pebbles and stow colourful stones in our canoes. We spend hours scouring the riverbanks, flood plains and ridges, turning up everything from wild raspberries and blueberries to animal tracks and antlers. Shortly after settling at a new camp, several people see a hummingbird — a rare sight this far north. A large cow moose and her yearling calf have installed themselves in a marsh across the river since we arrived.

August 1 — With twelve of us scanning the landscape constantly, wildlife sightings are a highlight of each day. Our trip poet encountered four wolves on a barren plain, but without trees for scale it took him a while to realize that his fierce-looking adversaries were in fact four-month-old wolf pups. A moose foraged in the shallows next to camp before dawn one morning. We watched a caribou ford the river and shake the water from his fur in a spray backlit by the setting sun. Peregrine falcons screamed from the tops of cliffs, and ptarmigan wandered among the tents, punctuating the night silence with their startling call.

Haruko, Joyce and Michael — our trio of artists — continue to find materials and ideas to inspire their work. Haruko gathered roots and made plaster casts of wolf, moose, Dall sheep and woodland caribou tracks. Joyce's sketchbook is filling up, and she continues to outpace everyone with her high-speed mountain ascents. Michael is our trip rockhound, picking up and examining countless stones, and carefully selecting a few each day to add to his collection.

*Tetlit Gwich'in elders from Fort McPherson prepare a feast of fresh moose meat
on a bed of willow branches at the confluence of the Peel and Snake rivers.* Fritz Mueller

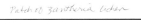
Patch of Xanthoria lichen

May & Elaine

Michael, Joe & Blaine

Braided section. Low water channel selection and a few areas of bottom scrape-age. An excellent day of sun and views of spectacular peaks. Lots of good campfire people pics with the polaroid. Grey talus, reddish bands - Light shows that once again reveal the valley light & shadow game and hidden trees. Cleared off to become an insanely gorgeous sunset with clouds/skies of orange cloud spectacular. Elaine went out to catch grayling and we had a wee feed of that at midnight. I love my little tent perch.

Pages from Joyce Majiski's Wind River journal provide a glimpse into the artistic process.
Joyce Majiski

Donald Standfield

Yesterday we woke to a light dusting of snow on the peaks, and now there's a bracing chill in the air as if autumn is around the corner. Today we paddled over six hours into a strong headwind and still covered fifty river kilometres. But it was a playful river day, featuring chutes and rapids, bouncy sections, wide sweeping turns and lots of spray.

August 4 — Our days seem to pass so quickly now, and a sense of urgency is taking hold. We are seeing such a dramatic change in the landscape as we make the transition from mountains to plateau. Leaving the mountains behind, we float past eroded cutbanks thick with drunken black spruce and gravel bars carpeted with wildflowers — goldenrod, monkshood, yellow paintbrush and fireweed.

The landscape is affecting everyone, but the significance of place has deepened for us in recent days. After a tiring day of paddling, we drew in to camp at the confluence of the Wind and Little Wind rivers. Our companion, May Andre, is from Fort McPherson, and this trip down the Wind has been an emotional pilgrimage for her. It was on the Little Wind that her father, John Robert, was born over ninety years ago, and where her Gwich'in ancestors lived year-round. She tells us about the life they led and the kind of people they were, and is so excited to make her first visit to this area. Just downstream, we came to Hungry Creek and Mount Deception, an area where our other Gwich'in paddler, Elaine Alexie, overwintered with her family twelve years ago.

As we move from mountains to Peel Plateau, the landscape physically changes, but so too does the story of the people who live here. We have entered the traditional territory of the Tetlit Gwich'in. Some of us miss the mountains, but others feel closer to home as the Wind River grows faster, wider, siltier.

August 7 — "Well, that was like fitting a well-fed boa constrictor into a wet girdle." Vancouver artist Haruko Okano had us in fits of laughter as she described packing up her tent during a morning downpour. Spirits are high on the Wind River, and an uncharacteristic day of rain cannot dampen anyone's mood.

Drawing closer to the Peel, the Wind ceases to be an intimate mountain river. The final braided sections are swift and shallow, and the river constantly cuts new channels and sweeps trees downstream. As we enter the Peel Canyon — a fifteen-storey-high gorge lined with rippled black walls — the sound of an engine steals our solitude: a passing floatplane tips its wings, the first sign of people in two weeks.

A sleepiness sets in on the Peel. The river is broad and brown — a giant, fluid conveyor belt — and we miss the fast, clear, exciting waters of the Wind. Holding a blue tin mug to his ear like a conch from the sea, Northern Tutchone elder Jimmy Johnny says, "Do you know what I hear? It's the Wind River saying, 'Come back, come back.'"

Rendezvous festivities at the Peel's confluence with the Snake River shakes us from our river reverie. We are met by celebratory gunshots and boatloads of revelers who have travelled all day from Fort McPherson to be here. Beaming Tetlit Gwich'in elders meet us on the beach, welcoming us for tea and a feast of country foods. Willow branches and spruce boughs are spread on the ground, tarps are raised and fires stoked. A dozen Gwich'in women prepare food while pots of tea boil. Three boatloads of Gwich'in men go to retrieve and butcher a moose shot upriver. A hundred people gather for celebratory speeches under flapping tents, in defiance of a relentless windstorm, embracing the Gwich'in hospitality and their appeals for conservation planning in the Peel watershed.

Nameless Hours — *Yukon Series, oil on canvas, 44" x 58."* Ron Bolt

The Timelessness of This Place

RON BOLT

It's a layover day today, with no loading of rafts, no hard pushing and shoving off the shallow river boulders. A hike is proposed into the nearby mountains, but the three artists of the group decline, citing the need for working time. I start a watercolour and make a mess of it, getting trapped into chasing the rapidly changing light and the constantly shifting clouds. Every trip is the same. The first work is stiff and clumsy. It's best to get it out of one's system as soon as possible. The brush-and-ink drawings are better. Tomorrow I will break through and pick up simple subjects using large brush work. Did a drawing in the camp journal and added four lines of poetry by William Blake that seem quite appropriate for this time, this place, this space:

> To see a world in a grain of sand
> And a heaven in a wild flower
> Hold infinity in the palm of your hand
> And eternity in an hour

This is perfect. It expresses the timelessness of this place, the microscopic world at my feet related to the macrocosm rolling off into the distant horizon.

Snake River, *ink and drybrush.* Ron Bolt

At right:
Snake River sketch. Ron Bolt

Opposite page:
Yukon Navigators, *2003,*
oil on canvas, 36" x 43." Ron Bolt

Rafting the Coal.   Coal River sketch by Helen Hoy, photo by George Smith

Fire on the Coal

GEORGE SMITH

S ays Peter, "Hey, George, come raft the Coal River with us in August. The place is beautiful. The river is wild. Some of your Kaska Dena friends will be coming. Even Tom King, the funny guy who created *Dead Dog Café* for CBC Radio, will join us. It should be fun."

Says me to myself, "Right! I should be excited about this. But how much fun will a place be that's named after something black that could lead to an ugly open-pit mine?"

On the other hand, I had been hearing about the little-known Coal River for years from my wilderness buddies. Kayaking on the Upper Coal in the southeast Yukon is a hot secret. The pools and mineralized terraces at the Cool Springs ecological reserve are rare and fascinating. The canyons near the south end in British Columbia are eye-poppers.

What really piqued my interest, however, was the chance to see the wildlife corridor. On maps, the Coal River Valley provides a critical wilderness link between the animal-rich Muskwa–Kechika in northeast British Columbia, through the boreal forests in the Yukon, to Nahanni National Park in the Northwest Territories. I wanted to see if this was real. So, says me to Peter, "I'm in."

What I didn't know then was that the Coal would teach me something about the importance of wildfire to wildlife in the Canadian boreal forest.

In late August our small plane flew northeast from Watson Lake, British Columbia, further into the heart of Kaska Dena territory in the Yukon. We were soon looking over a broad fire-altered landscape. Erratic swaths of tall spiky tree snags bleached white by the northern sun were sprouting above regenerating shrubs and young trees among patches of mature, unburned green forests. We were observing the 20-year-old impact of the "A Fire," one of the largest in Canadian history, which started in BC's Liard River Valley and raged through parts of the Yukon and the Northwest Territories.

Travertine terraces at Coal River hotsprings.
George Smith

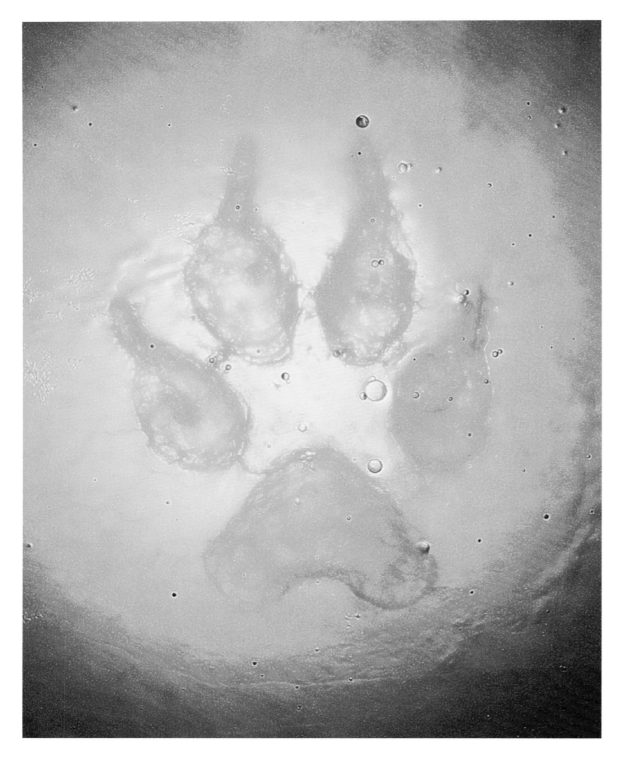

While the pilot was taxiing away from our drop-off about halfway up the river, I spotted the first signs of wild-life resilience on the gravel and mud spit. Near the edge of the water a set of fresh bear tracks wound around the prints of a moose. As we bushwhacked down the edge of the river to our raft put-in spot, more moose and bear prints were confused by the tracks of a medium-sized wolf.

And so it went during our six days on the river as we paddled through the heavily burnt upper section and the older forest lower down in BC. The large predatory birds — eagles, hawks, ravens and osprey — were plentiful, but most animals were seen only occasionally, since we tended to travel during their midday resting time.

We saw tracks along the river on virtually every sand or mud flat. Moose signs were ubiquitous, while wolf, grizzly, black bear and Canada goose tracks were common. Denis Porter, who had grown up in the area, delighted in finding deer, beaver, otter, mink and fox signs as we floated past his Kaska family trapline.

There was no doubt that the Coal watershed provides a vibrant wildlife highway enriched by tasty young shrubs, tree shoots and other nutrients released by fire and prized by ungulates and other plant-eaters. In turn, the abundant prey were obviously sustaining an active predator population.

And so I was a happy camper by the end of our trip. I felt reassured that the Coal River really was one of the key wildlife connectors that could help ensure that the western Canadian boreal forest community would have an opportunity to survive well beyond our lifetimes. It is now up to us all to make certain that land designations ensure that lasting vision.

Wolf track cast in amber:
a wolf as seen from below by Mother Earth.
Amber by Gwen Curry

Home away from home in the boreal forest.   CPAWS / Peter Sandiford

Courtney Milne

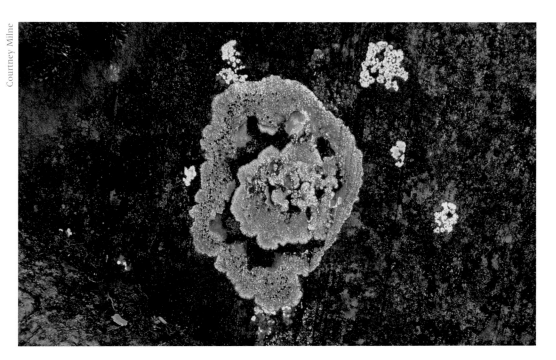

Snippets from a Bonnet Plume River Diary

COURTNEY MILNE

July 22 — Bonnet Plume Lake is larger than I had imagined — long and narrow, with a small tributary leading into the Bonnet Plume River. The campsite and surroundings are spectacular — mountains on all sides, ever-changing light, mist, a bit of rain while pitching our tents at the lake front. While waiting for the others we watched a bull caribou with a beautiful rack through Juri's spotting scope. First caribou I have ever seen in the wild!

July 23 — At breakfast Juri announced a seven-hour hike up and around the mountain above us. I deliberated, then met Gwen on the beach. She also was experiencing some hesitation. We decided to spend the day in the canoe. Should mention that dawn mists were fabulous and I did two to three rolls with the changing light — scenics and

reflections! We packed lunches and headed over to the camp across the lake, complete with a gorgeous log cabin, a smokehouse, and patch of wildflowers that I could die for. Did a few shots with the point-and-shoot, including a wonderful woodpile that glowed blue-green from the sun on the tarpaulins.

July 24 — Our camp is strewn out along the river and on a bit of a slope, so sleeping is an exercise in trying not to slide out the tent door. We did a hike to the slide area and six of us made it to the clear blue lake — freezing cold but a highlight of the trip so far. All but Richard doffed our clothes and made the plunge — absolutely terrifying and exhilarating! I was first in and Peter got shots of me with two thumbs up as I treaded the icy water — my best shot of the trip so far was into the sun-golden light with Kathy and George in profile, looking at each other, and Juri tucked in below doing his "amateur sketch" of the hills. I love it here. I am at home. My heart is singing; this river is a very special place. My task is to go beyond the documentary — to express the special nature of nature — the Supernatural. Tonight I did!

Courtney Milne

Courtney Milne

July 26 — Breakfast was porridge and eggs, then a frantic look for my journal, which seemed not to be anywhere and remained lost throughout the day. Also broke the small strut that holds up half the front overhang on the tent but managed to put it all back together by whittling a willow branch and adding a sleeve from my tent repair kit. The water was rough today, and we had our first portage of about 200 metres. Quite an ordeal carrying the huge rafts fully inflated along the narrow trails.

July 27 — A strange twist today saw us making very few gains on the river but a wonderful day of catch-up and photographing closeups of rocks. The rapids that we expected to check, then run, proved to be trickier than Juri had experienced before and actually were really vertically too narrow for the rafts to negotiate. They gave us about a one percent chance of success, which meant we had another portage — totally unexpected.... Because of the rapids, the river is loud here — churning and making its presence known. Threatened rain several times today, but nothing serious fell. Just as I thought I was finished I spotted a large rock face — multicoloured and very Kandinsky-ish (see opposing page.)

July 28 — Another big lesson is not to go to dinner, especially "late light" ones, without camera and tripod. The clouds momentarily turned bright gold and I wasn't there in time.

July 29 — In spite of the on-and-off rain spats, I found myself doing thoughtful, well-composed, lyrical compositions and worked with reflections in the puddles on the rocks. It really doesn't get any better than this — textures, archaic shapes, ancient feel, contrasting elements, graphic designs. Then, when I thought I had done it all, Juri sauntered by and mentioned blood-red pools at the point. On my way to find them I passed a rockslide with large and small pieces of shale-like rock, angular and clean-cut lines. I almost passed by, then realized that between the slabs were the most magnificent rock gardens of tiny plants, caribou moss, lichen, and amazing patterns of white lichen on chocolate-brown stone.

It felt in many ways like a sacred place and a sacred moment . . .   Courtney Milne

July 30 — Evening (10:30 p.m.) light was golden, thus moody blues, and I stayed at the river until 11:00, watching and recording. People seem very pleased to be here at this spot. As Juri says, it's a nine out of ten, with stream, fishing, wildlife, shelter, grandeur, mountains, light, and a grand view of the alluvial fan (below). A mother grizzly and her two-year-old cub were reported by the canoeists. Our folks saw only the rear end of the mother, and by the time I dove for my 300mm I saw nothing. Did however enjoy saying hello to a black wolf across the stream on the flats, who came to check us out then quickly disappeared. Two gray jays chased each other around the branches of two dead spruce and the stream continues to gurgle and babble in a most friendly, inviting way. Time to slow down here. Many flashbacks of earlier days of my youth [Milne grew up in Saskatoon].

July 31 — Very eventful morning. The sun burst forward and I hit the front lines on my belly — rain pants and rain coat, photographing the remains of the daisy-like flowers with their delicate whiskers, 300mm lens wide open into the sun and into the silver-studded brook...Robert has sighted a grizzly, which is swimming across the river to our side. I grab the tripod, F4 and 300mm. As it emerges from the river it looks more like a moose with its big humped back. I get several shots of him galloping across the flats before disappearing into the willows. He fits nicely into the tiny rectangle that indicates the area for spot metering, but what the heck — all part of the drama of the day. Then Robert spots another grizzly (with his naked eye) across the river, and later finds two caribou high on the mountain slopes. He also sees two of our group poised at the very pinnacle of the mountain, and three more on another slightly lower summit. What an eye that guy has. No binoculars, no glasses — just aware of movement. He jokingly says to me: "See that far mountain? There's a rabbit on it." I almost believe him!

Dave and Paul caught ten fish and they were fried in an egg and flour batter with oregano, as hors d'oeuvres. The main course, which we all ate under the tarp with a really ugly cold, wet wind, was a curried rice and veggie dish. Richard was sent to his tent to get out of his wet clothes, which he had put on in the hopes of his body heat drying them out! Much laughter.

August 2 — This has been a nine-roll day and though it is only 8:39 p.m., I am totally exhausted. I feel like hitting the sack but know that from here on in the pace is likely to be just as grueling. Both Gwen and I claim we feel old today. I am sitting on a rock at the edge of the river where Rapitan Creek spills into the Bonnet Plume. We are about 25 or 30 km short of Margaret Lake, where we'd hoped to get to for tonight and to have what would have been the last of the two-night stays. Instead we have a quick stay here and one-nighters from here on in. I am falling in love with this place and already it feels we are sliding into a time warp where the "Gathering" will be upon us before we are prepared to end this journey.

Red, white and Bonnet Plume blue on boreal green in the Great Northwest.   Courtney Milne

August 4 — This morning dawned rainy and cold — quite a miserable time getting the tent down and packing five pairs of socks that did not have time to dry on the line. Breakfast was hurried and with the difficulties of packing up in the rain, we weren't on the river until a little after 10:00. I slipped on the steep slope of boulders and went flying with a heavy pack on top of me — nothing injured except my dignity. By noon the clouds began to break, and I did more rock close-ups on a gravel bar at lunch. As we continued in the afternoon, the weather turned sunny with fabulous cloud formations. We were all a bit giddy. I was shooting with the 15mm and the 16mm fisheye and loving the effects. The water seemed even faster as we set out to do 40 km for the day. We decided to make an Olympic and world record by paddling as fast as possible during downhill stretches of water. We hit 19 km/hr and swear tomorrow we can do 20 km/hr. Kathy used her GPS to check our speeds.

August 5 — This day was the earliest start of them all. At 4:15 I couldn't stand it any longer lying there and watching the southern rim glowing orange, so I got up and struggled to where I had left the tripod and Pelican case beside the river (high bank). This dawn was spectacular. Black ominous clouds reflected in the river with a mere strip of open sky that shone orange and then wisps and patches of pink and mauve. The most exciting was the look through the 15mm wide angle. It shifted the proportion of dark tones to look more threatening. I worked for three-quarters of an hour, out to the point and back....

The afternoon drifted by quite lazily and we were soon seeing the black cliffs — our first glimpse of the Peel River Valley and our goodbye to the Bonnet Plume. It felt in many ways like a sacred place and a sacred moment. We were all together and fell into a deep silence — no paddling. After a brief celebratory feast on chocolate, we drifted down the Peel, where I did most of the pictures of that day. We were all quite awestruck.

Maelstrom moment, Bonnet Plume River.
Courtney Milne

The black cliffs turned to great patterns of stratified rock, and though I had only one roll of film readily accessible in my pocket, I made the shots count. One of the best images of the trip is of Jane and Sarah (the "chicks with sticks") cruising along in the green canoe (see page 57) with a massive cliff face lined with vertical white etchings rising high above them. I underexposed all the cliff faces by one f-stop.

August 7 — Once on the river, it felt wonderful to float, and this morning Kathy did not insist that we paddle. We even took a channel that the others had not, that put us in the shade under a mighty cliff with gold colouring against a jet-black coal face. It was without doubt one of the best shoots of the trip, and without the paddling I was able to work with relatively slow shutter speeds, doing dozens of variations of these colossal walls. Then Paul said, "Look up," and the trees at the top and the sky were another beautiful vignette — scattered cloud and blue blue sky with trees silhouetted. It did my heart good to have such a strong finish to the trip.

After the last bend and the last high wall, we see a white tent in the distance, and then more and more people, people, people. As we paddle into the gathering place on the mouth of the Snake River, they fire off seven or eight gunshots as a salute. There are far more people here than any of us anticipated. Two or three hours after our noon arrival, the Snake River group of two rafts and two canoes arrives, also to a fanfare of gun bursts. We all greet them. A lot of friendships have already been formed among the Yukon people. I circulate and try to get candids of people greeting people, including Larry Bagman, a very popular local Member of Parliament. Other boatloads of locals arrive, and shortly after the Snake River group, a party arrives with a moose and her calf and proceeds to prepare the meat.

I write this in my tent at the Gathering. It is raining now, though the rain did hold off for the ceremony of community people and river trippers. The temperature could very well fall to below zero tonight and put snow on the ground by morning. The winds were high and, during the speeches, it was the coldest weather of the entire trip. But it did not dampen the enthusiasm of the local people. They are highly charged and highly emotional about this project and what it is doing to raise awareness about the need to preserve and protect this land.

Nahanni —
Boreal Headwaters
of the World

HARVEY LOCKE

The South Nahanni River flows through one of the world's most stunning valleys. It combines granite peaks to rival Yosemite National Park, canyons that compare to those of the Colorado Plateau, with hot spring terraces and waterfalls that rival those in Yellowstone National Park. "Naha Dehe" is a place of special reverence for the Deh Cho Dene as well as a park of legendary significance to other Canadians, whether they are wilderness paddlers or armchair lovers of the romance of the North.

The original Nahanni National Park Reserve was set up to protect the river from hydroelectric development. The park's boundaries left out many of the area's extraordinary features as well as key wildlife habitat. It also failed to protect the entire watershed, which many Deh Cho Dene depend on for clean water. A wild valley of this beauty and cultural significance demands special treatment, nothing less than the national park that protects the entire watershed and all its marvels, so we mounted the Boreal Rendezvous trip with a crew we hoped would be worthy of the place and its future protection.

It was a diverse group that included Chuck Blyth, superintendent of Nahanni National Park, as well as Suza' Tsetso, a Dene cultural interpreter from Fort Simpson, Greg Yeoman, CPAWS NWT Conservation Director, and various others, including Justin Trudeau, his friend Gerry Butts, and a crew from CBC TV's *The Nature of Things*. We all piled into a floatplane in Fort Simpson for the two-hour flight in to the river. Just prior to landing we circled Virginia Falls — the place the Dene call "Naili Cho," meaning Big Falls — flew up the gut of the raging rapids of the "Sluice Box" and landed just upstream.

First one rainbow and then another appeared in the mist below where the river plunges 70 metres off a cliff split by a tower of rock. We paused to sit just upstream of the Sluice Box, the rapids above the falls where the Nahanni turns from a lazy river to a seething torrent. The last time I was at Virginia Falls

Rainbow at Virginia Falls. Harvey Locke

campground, a Dene who works for the park recounted in a campfire interpretive program that they hunt moose in the mountains and take meat out to their families on the boreal plain. After eating the rich meat, they return the bones to the mountains out of respect for the land and its gifts. As soon as we were settled, I quietly went off into the mossy forest by myself and made an offering of a piece of moose bone and antler velvet.

It was from a moose that my Dad shot thirty years ago in the Twitya–Keele watershed not far north of Virginia Falls. I vividly remember butchering the animal with him and eating its meat. Dad had kept the skull and velvet-covered rack. When he died I saved it from a trip to the dump, and this summer my son cleaned it up. It felt right to return a piece of it to these mountains.

A canoe trip that starts at Naili Cho begins with an ugly kilometre-long portage. Much of it is along an elevated and inclined boardwalk. The lower part is a greasy trail that descends to the river's edge through a set of steep switch-backs. It took several return trips for us all to move several rafts full of gear, two canoes, and what seemed like mountains of personal baggage.

As I was straining to control one particularly awkward and heavy load — a rubber-tired dolly burdened with sound and camera gear — things didn't seem very romantic. A poem came to me as I struggled to control the steel contraption and maintain my footing in the switchbacks:

The Northern Lights have seen queer sights
But the queerest they ever did see
Was Harvey Locke's folly
Dragging a dolly
Down the banks of the Nahanni

Above the brink of Virginia Falls, the Sluice Box rapid cascades past Mason Rock and into the legendary canyons of the Nahanni River.
James Raffan

There are four distinct canyons between Virginia Falls and the Nahanni's confluence with the Liard River. The area's first white explorers travelled upstream, so they named the canyons as they encountered them: First Canyon being the furthest downstream, while Fourth Canyon is furthest upstream.

At the first bend of Fourth Canyon, the Nahanni hurls its entire force at the base of an orange cliff. To be swept into it is disaster. Perched on our knees in the canoe, my partner, journalist Ed Struzik, steered an expert course while I paddled like hell. We ferried like mad across the riffles upstream to avoid disaster. As we splashed through, the standing waves slopped water harmlessly onto the canoe skirt that we had stretched over the top of the boat to keep it from being swamped. But then we settled in under our spray skirt to enjoy the glittering red, gold and green canyon walls.

*Below Third Canyon,
the gate of the Nahanni
is guarded by Pulpit Rock.*
Harvey Locke

Below Fourth Canyon we were carried along by the swift Nahanni current, doing light duty with our paddles. We spotted a white Dall's sheep on a ledge in False Canyon. Engrossed in conversation, Ed and I steered past a ledge and into some standing riffles. Unbeknownst to us, trouble was afoot.

While chatting away, we drifted broadside into huge waves. All it would have taken to escape was a smart draw stroke or two, but I wasn't thinking. Without warning, we flipped and found ourselves immersed in the river, canoe over our heads. We had to kick our feet free of the spray skirt to avoid drowning. "Thank God for Velcro" was all I could think at the time.

The alarm went out, and the rafts swept toward us in the swift-flowing water. Using a technique our guide "Nahanni" Neil Hartling had taught us in an earlier safety briefing, my wife, Wendy, hauled me up by the lifejacket into one of the rafts. Neil's crew pulled Ed to safety.

Fortunately, nothing was lost. Our waterproofed gear was securely tied in the canoe. Our cameras in their Pelican cases were fine as well. Ed, a veteran paddler of northern rivers, was most gracious about my error and did not seem upset by national television catching him being pulled unceremoniously out of the river.

As we paddled along Third Canyon in the deep shadows of afternoon, great terraced cliffs of brown and green towered above us, giving the illusion of mountains when we were really in a deep gorge cut into a plateau. It's as pretty a stretch of water as I've ever paddled. But nothing had prepared me for the emotional impact of the Gate of the Nahanni.

Suddenly, impossibly, the river turned at right angles and sliced straight through a vertical wall. And there, illuminated in golden light in the heart of the shadowy gorge, was Pulpit Rock, a monument of stone that stands off from the base of the cliff in the river.

For most of its 500-kilometre length, between canyons, the Nahanni flows gently through a forested valley. After First Canyon it winds in great loops through a broad forested valley before joining the Liard River on the boreal plain. From there the boreal forest spreads like a green cloak all the way to Labrador.

Some of these trees are substantial — some spruce, for example, are more than 60 centimetres in diameter. And throughout the river's length there is a healthy mosaic of forest stages, typical of a forest that has evolved with fire as a natural condition. Some areas are black with charred tree spars and bright with purple fireweed; others are thick with a forest of young birch; still others feature an even forest canopy whose moist environments support horsetails, as well as wintergreen and orchids that bloom at the foot of mature spruce trees. No forest fire suppression has ever occurred here. Chuck pointed out the value to scientific study of such a vast, unmanipulated, fire-evolved ecosystem.

It was a great pleasure to be out with people such as Suza' and Chuck, who know Nature. At sunset one night, Suza' looked up at the wispy pink clouds above the Headless Range: "See the cloud in the west? That means hot. See that cloud to the north? That means wind. Tomorrow will be hot and windy."

Hot and windy it was as we entered Deadman's Valley. Here, flowing down through a great rift in the upthrust rock of the Headless Range, enters Prairie Creek. Once through the ramparts of the north wall of the Nahanni, Prairie Creek spreads out over a huge alluvial fan before trickling into the main river. Twenty kilometres up this pretty little creek, just outside the existing boundary and hanging like the Sword of Damocles over the park, is a proposed silver mine about which we should all be concerned.

It was brought to the edge of production in the 1970s by the Hunt brothers of Texas. Mercifully, their scheme collapsed and the mine never opened. But sitting on a gravel bar on the banks of Prairie Creek is a legacy of this gamble: decaying 45-gallon drums of cyanide that could leach into Prairie Creek and then into the Nahanni River at any time. This almost entirely pristine watershed is no place for a mine.

Our last night on the river was one to test any camper. Suza''s prediction of hot wind persisted. Camped on a sandy beach in sight of the long rampart of Twisted Mountain and the turtle-like dome of the west side of Nahanni Butte, a wicked wind rose and whipped sand into little dunes on the floor of our tents. It was simply too hot to keep our tent doors zipped shut. Some tents flapped uncontrollably, others we thought might blow right away.

I awoke with a nose full of sand to the alarming sound of a canoe scraping along the rocky beach. Naked, with no time to dress, I jumped out of my sleeping bag and ran to catch it. There, walking along beside it, was Nadine, our filmmaker. She was staring in wonder as the canoe, driven by the wind, headed for the river. She had been up for hours, having been awakened by the sound of the footfalls of wolves beside her tent. (Verified when she pointed out their tracks.)

This was Nadine's first camping trip, and she had been mesmerized by the experience of the storm. She wasn't complaining about the surreal experience of a sleepless night among wolves or even of a morning in which a naked man chased a canoe down a beach in a dust storm. She was entranced by the transformative quality of wilderness. Her only thoughts were about when she could return. Watching Nadine being touched by the magic of the Nahanni reminded me that we must protect wild nature in places like this, not only for its own sake, but for the sake of ourselves, so that we might know what it is to be fully alive.

Prairie Creek Silver Mine just north of the river and outside the current boundary of Nahanni National Park. Decaying drums of cyanide have been stored here since the 1970s.
James Raffan

Black Bear on the Nahanni

WENDY FRANCIS

At the end of our third day on the Nahanni River, my husband, Harvey Locke, and I are sharing a canoe. I'm in the bow, while he paddles the stern. We are the last paddlers to pull up to our chosen camp, a gravelly beach on the right-hand side of the river. Just as we are about to land, I spot a dark object moving up the opposite shore, about a hundred metres downstream. I focus my binoculars on it. "Harvey — black bear!" I call over my shoulder. Our friends on the shore also have spotted it. We land our canoe, and I quickly run up the beach to share my binoculars with the others. We stand in awe, watching the beautiful small bear work its way up the shoreline, nosing the gravel beach and bushes along the way.

Black bears, found only in North America, are distributed widely across the continent, from the southeastern United States to Alaska and down into Mexico, and all across Canada. They live in forested landscapes, and once occupied virtually the entire continent except for the central Arctic. Now, they have disappeared from much of eastern and central U.S. and southern Canada (roughly sixty percent of their original range) because forests have been permanently cleared for agricultural production. While it is difficult to calculate total black bear numbers with precision, it is estimated that the continental population is somewhere between 300,000 and 500,000 animals.

Canada's first couple of conservation: Harvey Locke and Wendy Francis. CPAWS / Gerald Butts

So far, the bear hasn't spotted us; the wind is blowing our way. But suddenly he lifts his head and looks directly across the river at us. His ears are so big and round, they're almost comical. Then, surprisingly, he steps into the river and starts to swim across to our side! His black head, with its Mickey Mouse ears, bobs up and down as he paddles across the current. Every once in a while, he lifts his head and looks at our group.

As with all bear species, female black bears produce an average of two cubs approximately every two years, but only if food supplies are adequate. When food is scarce they can go as long as four years without giving birth. An average female will produce no more than ten to twelve cubs, often fewer, during her reproductive life. Many of those will not make it to adulthood, and only a portion of those will become mothers themselves. Bears' relatively low reproductive rate compared to other animals means their populations are sensitive to excessive killing by humans. Roughly ten percent of the North American population is killed each year through legal hunting. Other causes of death include highways and railroads, poaching, and wildlife management actions (such as killing a bear that has wandered too close to residential neighbourhoods).

Logo on Algoma Central Railway car heading north from Sioux Ste. Marie. From the canyons of Nahanni to Agawa, the black bear gets around in the boreal.

James Raffan

We are excitedly whispering among ourselves as the bear swims across the river, wondering what he is up to. The current carries him downstream as he swims, and he is out of sight, several hundred metres down the shore, by the time he lands on our side of the Nahanni. With nervous giggles and joking, we begin to unload the rafts and canoes. We are supposed to find our tent sites in the bushes toward the forest down the beach, but none of us wants to get that close to what might be the bear's path. I am listening intently as we work, half expecting to hear him come crashing out of the willows at any minute.

Bears are opportunistic feeders who eat a wide variety of foods, from insects and larvae to twigs, leaves, roots and berries. They also eat fish, carrion (animals killed by other means), and occasionally chase down and kill other animals themselves (like moose and deer calves). Eating is the most important activity in a black bear's life. Because they hibernate from November to March each year, they have only five to seven months a year to eat. They're large animals that need a lot of food, so it's important that they find the best quality of food possible.

Our host, Chuck Blyth, Superintendent of Nahanni National Park Reserve, stands like a sentry between us and the bear's potential paths. I ask him if it's okay to set up our tent in the willow bushes. I heed his reply to "wait a bit" with great respect. As Chuck moves away from the river toward the hillside behind the camp, several of us follow him. Our beach tends gently upward, away from the river, then slopes down again toward a depression that obviously is filled by the river during times of high water. Across from the depression is a steep, forested slope. One of our compatriots scouts down the depression to the left. He returns to report that he has encountered water not far away and that across that backwater are cliffs. We realize we are on what essentially is a small island with a bear! The bear will have no choice but to travel within a few dozen metres of us if he wants to continue moving upstream on our side of the Nahanni.

Bears — both black and grizzly — are wide-ranging animals. In their annual forays for food and mates, a healthy adult black bear can cover several hundred square kilometres. But its ability to do so successfully can depend on the condition of the area and the likelihood it will encounter people — especially people carrying guns. Bears are sensitive to human presence and development, though black bears are less so than grizzlies.

Even so, roads, buildings and human activity are often avoided by black bears. Logging is particularly harmful to black bears, since it removes the habitat they depend on and creates access roads, making bears more available to hunters. (Where clear cuts are smaller, are not sprayed with herbicides, and leave sufficient tree cover, cutover lands can be beneficial to bears for the berry crops they produce.) The more roads, logging, building, and human activity that occur on a landscape, the less of it is available for bears to use.

This phenomenon is called fragmentation — because of roads and development, a landscape is divided up into smaller blocks that are not large enough to meet a bear's needs for food and interaction with other bears. Within the boundaries of Nahanni National Park Reserve, bears are free to wander without encountering such obstacles. But the long, narrow shape of the reserve means bears often leave its boundaries, where they may encounter mining activities, roads or other development.

I decide to find a flat patch of sand on which to erect our tent (right). Normally, I like to allow sufficient distance for privacy between us and our neighbours. Tonight, our tent is within metres of Suza''s, Nadine's and Peter's tents.

Greg's and Patti's also are nearby. As I work at erecting the tent, I hear excited voices from up the beach. The bear is back! Our friends, who had waited patiently with Superintendent Chuck, were rewarded when they spotted the bear by some bushes a few dozen metres away, still moving in our direction toward the dry river bed.

Despite a reputation to the contrary, black bears are seldom dangerous to people. Research into bear attacks shows that while black bears often will bluff or charge, they rarely attack, and the injuries from such attacks are minor compared to those of grizzly bears. (There are, of course, exceptions to this, such as when a bear has become habituated to human garbage or a hiker inadvertently surprises a mother bear and her cubs.)

At Chuck's request, everyone steps back a few metres to give the bear room to pass. As soon as they do, the bear starts moving up river again. As I reach the group, he is trying to stay as far away from us as possible by crossing the steep forest slope across from us. Once he is past us, he drops down to the riverbank and trots rapidly away. For me, the experience is a reminder of what we must do if we are to continue to share wild places with such wonderful creatures: we need to understand and respect their need for room in which to live and travel. Silently, I thank the bear for teaching us this lesson and wish him well on his journeys.

Campsites are shared spaces. We are visitors among the local flora and fauna. "If we are to continue to share wild spaces with such wonderful creatures, we need to understand and respect their need for room in which to live and travel."
Wendy Francis

My Father's Smile

JUSTIN TRUDEAU

Pierre Trudeau at the base of Virginia Falls in 1970.

Peter Bregg (CP)

My family has always had a huge tradition of canoeing. It was something we did together from as far back as I can remember. Much has been made of my father's dual roles: intellectual and Prime Minister versus father. My brothers and I grew used to seeing both facets of him, except when we were canoeing. When we were off in the wilderness, he was just Dad.

Being away from the briefcases and the paperwork and the people who surrounded him most of the time, as we were when we canoed — those moments with him were probably the most precious of my entire life. And, in a sense, I've spent much of my life trying to reclaim how we used to feel when paddling together as a family, the way we all managed to feel when we got out there, away from the world of pressures and deadlines, and even time itself.

Because you completely lose track of time in the wilderness. For most of our trip on the Nahanni, I had no idea what day it was. I think it was by the third day of our trip — I'm not completely sure — that I was completely lost. If you'd offered me a million dollars to tell you what day of the week it was, I wouldn't have been able to tell you. I didn't have a clue. You get into a whole other rhythm when you're out there, as I'm sure many of you well know, living, as you do, surrounded by such incredible wilderness.

I loved paddling the Nahanni. It was absolutely beautiful. But one of things I should say now is that I loved the trip and the river not because my father loved the Nahanni and therefore I should love it, but because it embodied the same types of direct experiences with nature that we both love. He loved the massive canyons and the powerful river for the same reasons I do. Indeed, anyone who goes to the Nahanni, even for a day trip to the falls, will know that there's a smile that comes over your face — a smile born of the realization that there's something magical there. There is something extraordinarily precious about the Nahanni. And that is a thread that binds everyone who visits it, the thread that unites not just the people who live around it up here in the North, but people from all across the country.

Wilderness areas like this have the ability to bring people together in common cause. I would like to take this opportunity to mention and thank the Dene people who, through their direct connection to the Nahanni region, understand that the power and energy in the land is not just about electricity and oil, that it lies in the actual size and scope and purity of the land itself.

I think my father learned that when he paddled the Nahanni River back in 1970. One of the things people talked about on our trip was how my father was key in protecting the Nahanni from a power project, by creating the Nahanni National Park Reserve.

There's a famous picture of my dad — actually I saw it this afternoon hanging on the wall of the CPAWS office here in Yellowknife — in which he is standing just in front of Virginia Falls, thirty years ago. He's in his open-necked shirt and jeans and he's walking away from the falls with a funny little smirk on his face. Having paddled the river these last couple of weeks, and having been at Virginia Falls, and having talked about the park and the picture, I think I might have figured out what it was he was smiling about.

At the time he took that trip, he'd been Prime Minister for about a year and a half. But he had been a canoeist all his life. And he came up to see this place, this river he had read about and heard about for most of his life, the fabled Nahanni. And before he came here, you can bet that he was fully briefed on the economic benefits of the proposed hydroelectric power stations they wanted to build on the river, and how the cheap power from these would light up the North.

He'd likely heard all of that and more. But having paddled the river and carried his canoe around Virginia Falls — having got a real sense of the power of the place and the river — I think he was able to connect his passion for wilderness and his politics for the first time. As he reached down to take a drink from the river below Virginia Falls, then walked toward the camera with that silly little smile on his face, I think he realized, "I can actually do this. I can protect this river. The people of Canada have elected a canoeist as Prime Minister! They gave me the power to save this place." I think that's why he was smiling.

Right now, thirty years later, we have a chance, an amazing chance, with all the pieces in place, to finish that job. Let's all share that smile.

Adapted from a speech to the NWT chapter of the Canadian Parks and Wilderness Society in Yellowknife, NWT, on July 29, 2003.

Justin Trudeau at the base of Virginia Falls in 2003.
Harvey Locke

VP of Profound Thoughts on Canoeing

NEIL HARTLING

By any measure, Pierre Elliot Trudeau is a legendary Canadian figure, and perhaps his greatest attribute was his love of wild rivers. For wilderness lovers, his most notable achievement was the creation of Nahanni National Park.

I recall clearly an interview in 1971 with Prime Minister Trudeau. The interviewer asked the PM: If he could pick any career, apart from Prime Minister, what would it be? "Easy," he replied, "I would be an outfitter on the Nahanni River."

Nearly fifteen years later, not long after I'd started Nahanni River Adventures, I heard that he was retiring from office. I wrote to him and reminded him of his "dream career" and suggested that he might consider becoming a partner with me when he retired from politics. I'm not sure what I expected, but he sent me a personal letter saying he would consider it when he "really retired." Of course that day never came.

On reflection, I'm not sure what I thought his role would be in our partnership. When not involved in packing food, fixing gear, inviting other world leaders on trips, he likely would have been "VP of Profound Thoughts on Canoeing."

Outfitter Neil Hartling on boardwalk portage around Victoria Falls.
Wendy Francis

The "VP of Profound Thoughts on Canoeing" paddles Meech Lake in a birchbark canoe handmade by Algonquin builder Patrick Miranda. Bill Mason Productions

The Dease River is part of one of North America's largest river systems and lies entirely within the western boreal forest. Rising at Dease Lake, it cuts northeast through the rocks and till of the Cassiar Mountains before joining the Liard River at Lower Post and proceeding on to the Beaufort Sea via the Mackenzie River. Malcolm Edwards

LEG 2

Western Boreal

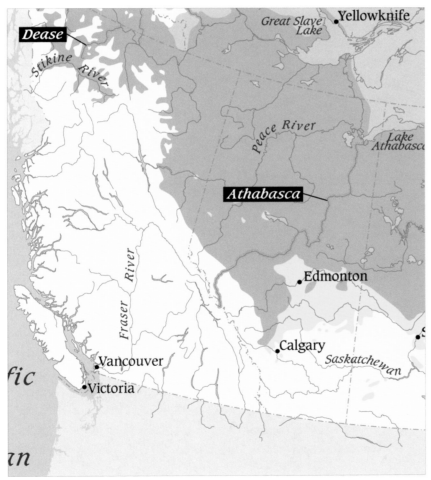

Chrismar Mapping Services

Being on the Athabasca River is kind of like a homecoming for me because we're flowing back to where I come from. I can just feel the presence of my people. In a sense, it's a rejuvenation for me. Travelling by canoe is an amazing experience. I've always travelled by motorboat. It is completely different. But now I'm glad I get to experience the river by canoe because it brings me back even closer to my ancestors.

MELODY LEPINE

Stikine — Spirit of Wilderness

WADE DAVIS

In the summer of 1879 John Muir went prospecting for glaciers, a journey that led him a thousand miles up the coast of British Columbia to Alaska and the mouth of the Stikine River. He disembarked at Wrangell, gateway to the interior, but was not impressed. Gold had been found on the lower reaches of the Stikine in 1861, and a later, richer strike further inland in the Cassiar had brought a rush of dreamers and drifters, thousands of miners whose presence stunned the native Tlingit and transformed Wrangell into a "lawless draggle of wooden huts."

Once upon the river, however, moving by paddlewheeler steadily through the islands of the delta, where eagles gathered by the thousands to feast on salmon runs so rich they coloured the sea, his mood shifted to delight. In every direction were signs of the wild. Immense forests of hemlock and Sitka spruce rose to soaring mountain walls adorned in waterfalls and ice. On canyon bluffs stood mountain goats, fearless as if innocent of human predation. Grizzly bear and white wolves walked the shoreline amidst clouds of cottonwood down. The entire valley, wrote a bedazzled Muir, was a flowery landscape garden, a Yosemite a hundred miles long. In a journey of but eighteen hours, he counted over a hundred glaciers.

Reaching Glenora, the tent settlement then at the head of navigation, Muir was keen to see more. As soon as opportunity permitted, he climbed Glenora peak, a rocky crag rising directly from the river to 7,000 feet. From the summit, this veteran of a thousand strolls in the Sierra Nevada looked west toward the Coast Mountains through which he had just travelled. "I never before had seen," he later wrote, "so richly sculptured a range or so many awe-inspiring inaccessible mountains crowded together." From this vantage, he tallied another 200 glaciers. With night drawing near, Muir recalled, "I ran down the flowery slopes exhilarated, thanking God for the gift of this great day." Returning to California, he would name his beloved dog Stikine, after this river of enchantment.

Standing today on the summit of Glenora, in an August snow squall, with raptors scraping the sky and ravens yielding to the ice, it is impossible not to think of this grand old man of conservation. His visit to the Stikine was fleeting, mere days, and what he saw of the river was but the lower third, arguably the most conventional. Had his eyes turned north and east, down the snowmelt gullies and past the tangled spruce, beyond the rivers, lakes and jagged peaks, they would have fallen upon uninhabited valleys larger than entire countries, a landscape where Canada could hide California and America would never find it.

What would he have made of the soaring plateaus of the Spatsizi headwaters, land of the Red Goat, a vast wilderness preserve aptly named the Serengeti of Canada for its immense herds of woodland caribou and stone sheep? Or the depths of the Grand Canyon, Canada's largest, where the Stikine disappears into the earth, a raging torrent that flows for more than 60 miles beneath cliffs of basalt and sedimentary rock rising 1,200 feet straight up from the river's edge? To the south of the canyon looms Edziza, Ice Mountain, sacred to the Tahltan Indians, a towering dormant volcano veiled perpetually in cloud and capped at 9,000 feet with an ice field eight miles across.

To reach Edziza from the north can mean crossing a lava field so rough that local guides sometimes measure distance not in miles, but in pairs of boots worn out by the effort.

The Stikine is more than a river; it is a wilderness of the spirit, a remote and wild, vibrantly beautiful homeland — a neighbourhood, albeit an odd one with more caribou than people, but a neighbourhood nevertheless, where man and nature have over the years come to terms with each other. And those terms involve a set of relationships to the land that demand the luxury of space. This conviction, never spoken about and never forgotten, hovers in the imagination of all those who call the Stikine home: guides and outfitters, trappers, homesteaders, bush pilots and above all the native Tahltan who comprise most of the population and whose presence gives meaning to the valley.

Mist, forest, pack horse and flat-bottomed skiffs on the Stikine: a riparian neighbourhood where people and nature have over the years come to terms with each other.
Wade Davis

Captain's Log — August 23, 2003

LAUREL ARCHER

It's happening. You're in Two Mile Rapids on the Dease River in far northern British Columbia, and you've missed your line. All you can do is straighten out the canoe with a King Kong pry and throw your torso into a full-on power stroke. The bow of your canoe drops into the corner of the ledge hole. *Whoosh!* And Leon Johnny, Kaska Dena elder, is wearing the largest wave in the river. Good thing he's taken off his hat for the descent.

Oh no, there's the gunwale grab! You brace with all your might, knowing that if you go over you will forever be the notorious canoe guide who swam, dumping a slender 73-year-old into freezing water on a chilly, late August day.

But the thousands of hours challenging yourself on the river in a kayak or canoe pay off. The boat stays upright, and Leon shouts, "Woo hoo! Woo hoo!" all the way down the wave train.

In the eddy on river right, Leon turns to beam at you. Water droplets hanging off his eyelashes behind his glasses, he says, "That was a big wave."

You exhale, finally, and then both of you are giggling like loons. In all his years of travelling the Dease, Leon has never paddled down the guts of Two Mile in a canoe, and now he has — though almost not!

Behind you, Malcolm Edwards and Jimmy Rankin make their line, but not without a soaking. You can tell by how they slosh into the eddy and by the size of Jimmy's eyes. As they come up side of you, he explodes, "Those waves are a lot bigger when you're in the canoe than they look from land!" He and Leon do a play by play of their descents, and Malcolm leans over to you and says with a smile, "Did you have a moment there?"

You grin hugely and say, "Did I ever!"

After the rush:
whitewater maven and
Kaska Dena elder
Leon Johnny.
Laurel Archer

At left: *The moving water that propels canoes down the Dease River is the same force that transports tons of sediment every second, cutting through river banks and reshaping the landscape.* Laurel Archer

Through Jimmy's Eyes

BRUCE HILL

Boreal troubador Jimmy Rankin. Laurel Archer

oming from a background of civil rights activism in the '60s in the United States, where music was a fundamental part of the struggle, I have often wondered why the environmental movement hasn't done more to bring together the complementary joys of music and wilderness. It seems like such a logical thing to do because we are, when we do it right, a singing species.

On the Dease River, Jimmy Rankin soaked up experiences like a sponge. Songwriters do that. I spent the six days watching Jimmy and his wife, Mia, handle the challenges and experience the joys of canoeing down one of Canada's magnificent boreal rivers. Their joy and innocence on the river confirmed a few things I've long suspected: that somehow, somewhere, we have lost sight of the fact that protecting wilderness is something that needs little justification; that while landscapes devoid of our depredations have endless scientific and cultural justifications, unmarred landscapes are also simply a necessary part of our national and cultural identity; that when we lose wilderness, our humanity is somehow diminished; and, finally, that we can't thrive as a species without wilderness, or without music.

And can Jimmy Rankin sing.

Shut your eyes and imagine a campfire along the banks of a broad, clean river in Canadian wilderness. Imagine a seemingly disparate group of strangers gathered around a crackling campfire, including an old Kaska Dena man, Leon Johnny, who has lived his life on the river and knows it intimately, two young Kaska Dena men trying to hold onto their culture, and a mix of guides, activists and general lovers of rivers. Imagine a clear boreal sky, with thousands upon thousands of stars, and the night sounds of the boreal. Then imagine a clear Cape Breton tenor soaring into that sky with wonderful images of longing and affirmation and love.

22.04.03

JR

Watercolour by Jimmy Rankin

Imagine sitting around the campfire wondering how life could be sweeter as folks wander off to their tents, sitting and talking quietly with Jimmy around the dying embers of a campfire when suddenly the northern sky lights up in a stunning display of the Aurora Borealis and curtains of light dance from horizon to horizon, framed by the dark shapes of mountains and boreal pine and spruce. It was that fine.

When Europeans and Asians first came to these lands several centuries ago, the assumption was that the riches were essentially limitless. We know that was an arrogant and wrong assumption. Much of what we found is gone — the cod from our oceans; the salmon from too many rivers, on both coasts; the old-growth trees of Ontario and British Columbia. Roads spread into wilderness in the frenetic search for resources to sustain a world that all evidence says cannot be sustained. Whales in remote waters die on barren shores poisoned by the effluents of our lifestyle.

But we are not so far from our past that we always forget our dependence on the land. We are not so far away yet that we cannot recognize the joy in someone's eyes as they first experience wilderness on a Canadian scale.

Hope was renewed on the Dease through the lens of clear waters and pristine forests, through the quiet dignity of Leon Johnny and his seventy years of living on the Dease, and through the honest and open eyes of Jimmy Rankin, who showed me the wonder and majesty of Canada's boreal forest again for the first time.

Curtains of light in a boreal sky. James Raffan

What's for supper? These great blue heron nestlings spend two months in their treetop home before they are ready to fly. Their growing appetites keep parents on a constant hunt for turtles, frogs, snakes, crayfish and small mammals. James Raffan

Nothing beats slow food on the trail.
Top left: *Mixing the sun's energy in wheat flour with water, lard, baking powder and salt to make simple bannock.* Top right: *Dough is rolled on cutting board or canoe. Add brown sugar, margarine, spices, nuts, raisins and a few bugs.* Left: *Twenty minutes in a folding campfire oven and* **voila!** — *the best cinnamon buns you ever tasted.* James Raffan

Food on the Trail

JAMES RAFFAN

We chat and putter as the meal takes shape — about home, about work, about the state of the universe. We could have opted, as some paddlers do, for boil-in-a-bag meals, but we would never have been able to carry enough to do us for even half the trip; or we could have gone for instant freeze-dried meals, which would have been light but very likely would have put us on the rough edge of nausea for most of the trip (not to mention filling our tents with noxious fumes on a regular basis); or we could have opted for cornmeal mush and bannock, which, along with a few supplementary items, would have sustained us nutritionally but been no fun to eat. And for sure, that diet would have denied us this kind of group banter around the details of preparation. Instead, we opted for the rather more elaborate eight-day menu that hits the middle on taste, weight, palatability and, unless someone adds too many dried onions, gets a low average score on the flattus index as well.

Food preparation is one of the boons of self-contained travel such as this. When people say that food tastes better on camping trips, they're really saying that they were hungrier than they might otherwise have been, and that they enjoyed the labour of preparing it under Spartan conditions. Camp food tends to taste like its packages, but camp cooking brings people together to share the simple pleasure of preparing, cooking, serving and cleaning up after a meal. You know where the food comes from, how it was cooked, who prepared it and where the uneaten portion goes, if there happens to be one, which is a rare event on this journey. Preparing our journey meals is an important social binder, a time to lift everyone's sprits and attentions back to the common cause.

From *Summer North of Sixty*, 1990

Chipewyan elder Eddy Catholique at a picnic lunch during a caribou hunt on the south shore of Great Slave Lake. On the menu: caribou tongue cooked in situ.
James Raffan

Boy tending a whitefish net on the Peel River at "Eight Mile" just south of Fort McPherson, NWT. James Raffan

Dancing Below the Surface

TOMSON HIGHWAY

The glimmering, emerald-green net stretched out.
Sunlight shining through the ice made it look like lace.
Seeing the net dancing nearby, trout, whitefish, even pike,
swam over to take a look.

ana ayapiy askihtakonahkosiw atámihk miskwamihk,
é-miyo-askihtakonahkosit. héy, é-miyo-nahkosit ayapiy ayis
é-sápónahkosit písim miskwamihk ómisi isi! ahpo
namékosak ékwa atihkamékwak ékwa iyinito-kinoséwak
pé-tahtakowak ta-pé-kanawápamácik.

English and Cree translations from the story "Fox on the Ice."

Illustration by Brian Deines

Entering the boreal for overnight camping requires careful planning of clothing and kit. Often what's left behind is as important as what's taken along. This colourful jumble of gear on a trail marks the spot where travellers bailed out for a refreshing swim below the falls that made the portage necessary in the first place. James Raffan

Sharing the wild. With 2,700 species of mosquitoes in the world, it's not suprising that several of them make the boreal home. On occasion, they become an unusual supplement of fresh meat and protein in a riverside cabbage and carrot salad. James Raffan

Thought to be sacred by some, the snapping turtle is Canada's largest freshwater turtle, with a shell that can reach nearly half a metre in length. An enthusiastic and successful carnivore of the southern boreal, they also eat a variety of aquatic plants and often live thirty years or longer in the wild. James Raffan

Herptiles (reptiles and amphibians) are an important indicator of ecosystem health. Frogs in particular, with their distinctive croaks, grunts, gurgles and quavers, are an important food source for otters and other carnivores but also a highlight of the boreal's summer chorus. When they are silent, the forest is in trouble. James Raffan

A Magical Place

DAVID SCHINDLER

Boreal wetlands provide critical habitat for many creatures but also act as giant sponges, filtering water before releasing it slowly back into the landscape, feeding the thousands of rivers that are sources of drinking water for many North Americans.

Linda Anne Baker

To me, the boreal forest is sort of the essence of Canada. To me, it's not just a forest with trees in it. I study the plumbing of the boreal, the rivers and lakes that drain the forest, and I know how they're affected when the forests are damaged. The wetlands that are part of that landscape shouldn't be forgotten, either. The boreal is sort of a magical place. There must be a thousand shades of green, yellow green, and grey green. And the low light and wetness really make those stand out.

The Invisible Forest Companies

DAVID SCHINDLER

In a typical year, forest fires consume about 25,000 square kilometres of the boreal. The fires are a mixed blessing — bad for forest companies in the short run but good for the forest in the long run.

Donald Standfield

A nd dry forests and warmer temperatures equal more forest fires. As a result, I think we're going to have fire, like an invisible natural forest company, competing with forest companies for trees, for those same forests. And then, of course, as we've recently come to realize, the removal of forests by oil and gas and expansion of towns and roads is like another invisible forest company. And then, as well, there are the visible forest companies.

An Ecological Guardian Angel

GREG YEOMAN

Boreal mushroom
Linda Anne Baker

T he Dene say, "We take care of the land, the land takes care of us." And they talk about the boreal forest as a
green halo across the northern part of the globe. I think of the boreal forest as an ecological guardian angel:
we take care of the boreal, the boreal will take care of us — with all the filtering of water, the storing of carbon,
the creating of oxygen, the regulation of climate. This is a major ecosystem, for the world.

For My Grandchildren

DAVID SUZUKI

Thank you to CPAWS and the Canadian Boreal Initiative for including the David Suzuki Foundation in this wonderful project. I am honoured to be a part of it.

I'm not as old as our William Commanda, who opened our evening tonight, but I'm now sixty-seven years old. The University of British Columbia kicked me out, kicking and screaming, two years ago, when I reached sixty-five. I'm now in the last part of my life and have been dragged into the ranks of elderhood.

But I have no hidden agenda. I'm beholden to no one. The only reason I'm up here talking to you is my three grandchildren. They never asked to be born into this world. I know that every generation has received a sacred trust from their ancestors. I'm here because I want to pass on this world to them in better shape than I found it in.

We received the planet from our elders, and it is our obligation to pass it on to future generations as we received it. And we haven't been doing that in this country for quite a few generations now. I see the Boreal Rendezvous as an opportunity in some small way to leave something there, something to remind us of what once was, and I hope may be again in the future.

I grew up in British Columbia in the late 1930s and early 1940s in a world that was fundamentally different from what it is now. You cannot imagine the enormous changes that have happened in my lifetime. Much of Africa and of South America had yet to be explored by industrial human beings, by the western world. Most forests of the planet were pristine. And the oceans were teeming with animals and plants that people were able to exploit. But we were dazzled, especially after the Second World War, dazzled by the enormous advances that were made by science and by the technological inventions that followed.

I remember after the war, in 1945, when our family moved to a farm in southern Ontario. We were told about a new wonder chemical that came out, and I remember my mother every night setting the dinner table, then taking the wonder chemical and spraying it over the table, where it settled on our food. The chemical was DDT. We thought that through science we could kill our pestilences, and that this wonder chemical was perfectly safe for human beings. History has proved otherwise.

CPAWS / David Dodge

What a dazzling array of technological advances have impinged on my life: we split atoms; we routinely go into outer space; we have computers that can beat human beings at chess; we have deciphered the entire genetic code. But I fear we've gotten carried away with how smart we are, how powerful we are. We've taken it on our shoulders to be responsible for the entire planet. Now we feel that it's an opportunity for us to exploit it as we see fit.

I think the beginning of this new millennium is a turning point. We can either continue on the suicidal path we're on, or we can begin to recognize that we belong to a much greater community, a community of organisms that make the planet habitable and make our lives possible.

That's what the boreal forest represents. This is the largest intact forest left on the planet. So we have an enormous opportunity here. We have no idea what a forest is. We don't know everything that belongs to a forest. We have a lot of people that call themselves foresters. They tell us they know how to manage a forest. When they talk about managing a forest, they are not even talking about a forest. They are talking about a plantation. A plantation is fundamentally different from a forest, and we don't seem to

Andrea Maenza

understand how it works. But we still have this gigantic forest that remains up there that is home to some of the most charismatic animals on this planet.

For most of my life, it has been my great dream to see a wild wolverine. I never have. I have never seen a marten. This is the home of grizzly bears, caribou, elk, and bison, as well as whooping cranes that nest up in Wood Buffalo National Park. This is an amazing ecosystem, and we still have a chance to do something to protect it and to learn how to live with it. We can learn from the people who are already living there and who have lived there for thousands of years.

Boreal Rendezvous is a great opportunity for us all. Since most Canadians live in cities in the South, we have very little knowledge of that great jewel that still exists in the North. And we're here to use the celebrity of people like Ken Dryden, Justin Trudeau, Silken Laumann and the others in this impressive list, to canoe parts of the river systems throughout the boreal so that we can celebrate this great forest.

Our aim through Boreal Rendezvous is to bring the boreal forest into the living rooms of Canadians, realize to make us aware of how wonderful it is and to fall in love with it. I hope that is what we will do — celebrate that we are part of this world, realize that the boreal makes the planet livable for us. It's the home of our brothers and sisters, other species, and we're going to protect it for my grandchildren and their grandchildren, too.

From a speech given at the launch of Boreal Rendezvous in Toronto.

Passport to a Dream

KEN DRYDEN

W e have a world map in our kitchen. I love to look at maps. I always love to imagine being in different places. Here was a chance to go into this area. To go into it with people who knew something about it and take in their experiences and their knowledge, as well as to experience just being on a river day after day. What does it look like, what does it feel like, what must it have been like, what would it be like in winter? I mean, once somebody asked me [to join Boreal Rendezvous], the answer was pretty easy.

Ken Dryden was one of many Canadians who took time out in the summer of 2003 to raise awareness about the importance of the boreal forest. CPAWS / David Dodge

Biologist David Suzuki and hockey legend Ken Dryden were part of the team who paddled the Athabasca River in support of Boreal Rendezvous. CPAWS / David Dodge

Guardian of the boreal, the common loon, the oldest bird in the bird book. James Raffan

Every river has its resident craft.
A riverboat on the Churchill River, with hull, stems, gunwales and seats made of boreal wood cut in mills throughout the forest. Laurel Archer

LEG 3

Central Boreal

R apids are a challenge. Dangerous though they may be, no one who has ever known the canoe trails of the North does not love their thunder and the rush of them. No many who has portaged around whitewater, studied the swirls, the smooth, slick sweeps and the V's that point the way above the breaks, has not wondered if he should try. Is there any suspense that quite compares with that moment of commitment when the canoe then is taken by its unseen power? Rapids can be run in larger craft, but it is in a canoe that one really feels the river and the power of it.

SIGURD OLSON — from *The Singing Wilderness*

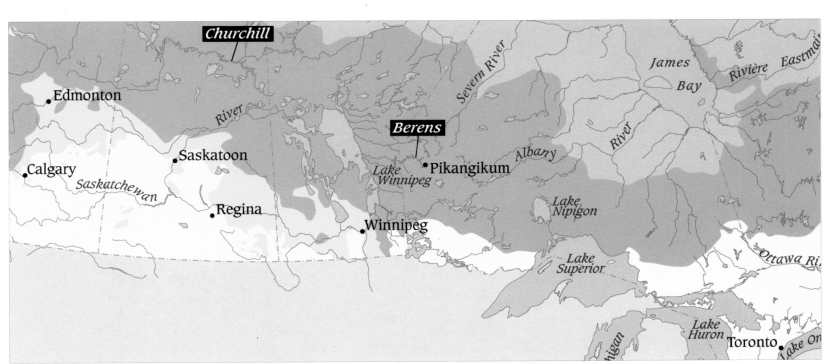

Chrismar Mapping Services

The Singing Forest

CANDACE SAVAGE

August 1 — From the dark wall of forest on the opposite shore, a clear flute-like voice pours out, wistful and melancholy. Pure sweet *Canada Canada Canada Canada*. The anthem of the boreal forest.

It's our first morning out as part of the Boreal Rendezvous, and our paddles have brought us here, to the shore of Wallace Island at the north end of Besnard Lake in central Saskatchewan. The sky glows softly with the silver light of dawn and, at my feet, silver water ripples against ancient rocks. Everything is enveloped in silence.

Anne Janssen of the Canadian Parks and Wilderness Society pads up beside me, her face still soft with sleep. "It's a white-throated sparrow," she says happily. The bird is hidden somewhere in the foliage, and when the notes ring out again, strong and wild and true, it's as if the song had risen from the very heart of the forest.

On the tongue of rock behind us, the rest of our party — a group of pavement-pounders-turned-wanna-be-voyageurs — are rubbing tired muscles and packing up their gear, preparing for a day of hard paddling down Besnard Creek and into the Churchill River. There is no sign that anyone else has heard.

If the boreal forest is singing to us — a song of abundance, beauty and hope — what will it take to make us stop and listen?

Red-tailed hawk
Marta Scythes

Canadians are a hardy northern people who by and large prefer to live as far south as we can. Yet even though relatively few of us actually live up north, the boreal forest — that seemingly endless scramble of rock, water and scraggy spruce — remains the bedrock of our national experience.

This is the iconic Canadian landscape, the inspiration of Tom Thomson, the natural habitat of Pierre Trudeau, the home of our bucktoothed national animal. From the outset of our national adventure, it has also served us well as the powerhouse of economic development. To the extent that our economy is based on the extraction of natural resources — first furs, then minerals, oil and gas, hydro power, lumber and pulp — the great north woods have been the source of much of our wealth. If the boreal forest can be said to be etched on our collective psyche, it is also the mark of our material success, a fact that is stamped on every loonie that jingles in our pockets.

Now comes word that this "Great Green North" is more important than we ever knew, and not just to Canadians, either. According to an analysis done by the World Resources Institute in the late 1990s, Canada's boreal is one of only three large, more-or-less intact natural forests that remain in the world; the others being the taiga (or boreal forest) of Russia and the North Amazon rain forests of Brazil. Although the southern fringes of the boreal have been heavily impacted by industrial development, the region is so vast and remote (not to mention buggy and cold) that much of it has been spared the effects of intensive human use. The result is a forest ecosystem that not only retains all of its life-sustaining functions — its ability to filter and purify water being high on the list

Opposite page:

Rich, moist conditions inside the boreal allow for all manner of biological activity, including opportunities for various symbiotic relationships between epiphytic lichens, such as old man's beard, and trees, like this aging black spruce. Marten Berkman

— but that also provides safe haven for its full, natural complement of plants and animals. In a world where species are now blinking out at the rate of three every hour, the survival of a healthy and vibrant ecosystem, lively and complete, is an almost miraculous rarity. And, as Canadians, it is ours to enjoy and to cherish.

And there is outside support for the Canadians that are beating the boreal drum. Conservation of Canada's boreal forest is also the driving passion of the new kid on the block, the Canadian Boreal Initiative. Formed in 2003, CBI is generously assisted by Pew Charitable Trusts, a family foundation based in Philadelphia. In addition to providing major funding for the Boreal Rendezvous, CBI has also invested in research that is designed to help us sense the colour and sparkle and life of this shadowy forest. Who knew, before they told us, that all that scrubby brush was really one big aviary that produced not millions, but billions, of birds every year? Listen up, Canada; listen up, world: the boreal forest is for the birds.

August 2 — We have two guides to lead us down the Churchill, Laurel Archer — the person who literally wrote the book on canoe travel in this neck of the woods — and Phil Roberts, a seventeen-year-old high-school student from a Cree village called Grandmother's Bay, who has been tooling around these waters since he was a kid. When I asked Phil how he got hired on as a guide, still so young, he said it was because he could be relied on "not to do anything stupid." But his qualifications run deeper than mere common sense. He's strong, he can read the river and he's a good hand in a canoe. He's also a keen observer: yesterday, he picked out the faint ochre lines of a rock painting on the shore of Besnard Lake that none of us had known was there.

This morning, when we were paddling through the maze of islands and channels that is Black Bear Island Lake, somebody called out to ask him to identify a flock of birds. He checked them with his binoculars and said that they were coots. But after we camped, I found him sitting on a rock, studying a guidebook to Saskatchewan birds that he had borrowed from one of the other paddlers. "They weren't coots; they were this one," he said, pointing to a grebe. "So many different kinds." So many!

Merganser
Marta Scythes

The research commissioned by the team of Boreal Initiatives was released in December 2002 in a report entitled the "Importance of Canada's Boreal Forest to Landbirds." ("Landbirds," as distinct from water- and shorebirds, is a catch-all grouping that includes hawks, owls, woodpeckers and songbirds, among others.) Authored by Peter Blancher, a former chief of the Migratory Bird Populations Division of the Canadian Wildlife Service, now on secondment to Bird Studies Canada, the study comes with impeccable credentials. Although the data on birds in the boreal region is sketchy and relies heavily on surveys in the southernmost forest fringe, Blancher has made the best of the available information and is satisfied with the overall accuracy of his conclusions. For the most part, his figures are "robust" and reliable, he believes.

In a nutshell, Blancher's analysis shows that the boreal forest is a treasure house of birds, an assertion he supports with a flight of numbers. For instance, when he tallied up the landbirds that breed in the boreal forest, the list turned out to include no fewer than 9 different species of woodpeckers, 10 different finches, 11 blackbirds, 15 flycatchers, 25 sparrows, 27 wood warblers, and on and on, for a grand total of 186 species in 35 families. And these are just the regular breeders: another 41 species show up now and then, bringing the number to 227, or almost 80 percent of the landbird species that occur in Canada.

It's not just that there are a lot of different kinds of birds flitting around in the bush. Many of those species are also extremely abundant. For example, Blancher puts the boreal-breeding population of red-eyed vireos at around 70 million birds, and it isn't anywhere near the top of the roster. The dark-eyed junco, a gnatty little slate-backed sparrow that shows up at southern feeders in spring and fall, may be the most populous species of all, with a count that may exceed 200 million. Taken together, Blancher estimates that somewhere between one billion and three billion landbirds nest in the boreal each spring. By fall, when their offspring have fledged and joined them on the wing, the number surges up to three billion to five billion. (This amounts to 60 percent of all the landbirds in Canada and 30 percent of the combined population of Canada and the U.S.) And when you think of the swimming and wading birds that rely on boreal lakes and bogs — all those coots, grebes, ducks, geese, loons, cranes, in their thousands and millions — it becomes clear that the importance of the region to birds cannot be overstated.

For certain species, the northern forest is all there is. These are birds such as the Palm, Tennessee and Connecticut warblers, which despite the southern affinities of their names, nest almost exclusively in the Canadian boreal forest. In fact, more than 90 percent of the global population of these three species breeds in our north woods, a distinction that they share with the northern shrike and the black-backed woodpecker. According to Blancher's calculation, there are another 35 species, mostly flashy little warblers and sparrows, that rely on the boreal forest to support at least 50 percent of their worldwide breeding population.

But what on earth are they doing here? This is the boreal forest we're talking about, not the Amazon. Isn't life supposed to falter and thin as you travel north? By rights, the boreal forest should support few species at low populations, and yet instead we find with this stunning diversity and abundance of birds. What is it about this forest that makes it so productive? And why, given its importance, is this the first we have heard about it?

The tiny black-capped chickadee weighs only a few grams but lives through the boreal winter, maintaining a body temperature similar to humans, without Polartec or Gore-Tex, only featherweight down of the finest kind.

Linda Anne Baker

August 3 — Today we took a long detour up the river to a place called High Rock Narrows. As the name suggests, the narrows are a tight, steep-walled channel, almost a gorge, between two islands of rock. Huge cubes of granite are piled heavily one on top of another to form the face of the cliffs, like blocks thrown down haphazardly from some gigantic fist. One member of our party, a Cree educator, confided that he had seen this place in a dream once, though he had never been here before. He said it was "big medicine." I didn't know that people actually used that phrase, but I did know what he meant. On the flat surfaces of the granite, some unknown hand in an unknown time had inscribed images: they showed strange, magical creatures and people brandishing rattles and sprouting horns. And there were pictures of birds, too, wonderful birds with long, serpentine wings that scrolled down like banners, framing a human figurine. Birds of power and mystery.

Canada goose
Marta Scythes

Fiona Schmiegelow is an assistant professor of Renewable Resources at the University of Alberta, a member of the Sustainable Forestry Management Network, scientific advisor to the Canadian Boreal Initiative and a passionate advocate for sustainable use and conservation of the boreal forest. She lives, breathes and sleeps boreal issues. But she remembers the time a few years ago when she decided to set aside her ambition of working in the cathedral forests of British Columbia and refocus her sights further north. "I expected the boreal forest to be sort of boring compared to some of the other forests I had worked on," she says, as though startled by the thought. "Like other people, I had to learn to appreciate it. Knowing what I do now, though, I think the boreal forest is pretty magical."

As Schmiegelow sees it, Canadians have tended to take the boreal forest for granted, as a familiar but distant backdrop to everyday life. And this attitude of benign neglect has extended to scientists, with the result that worryingly little research has been conducted in boreal ecosystems. "In many cases," Schmiegelow laments, "we don't even know the specific nesting requirements of quite common boreal species." So it's little wonder that we, John and Jane Q. Public, don't know much about northern birds, if the experts haven't been paying attention to them either. Yet whatever the gaps in the current knowledge, one fact is perfectly clear. The main attraction of the boreal for landbirds is the superabundance of food.

The key, as Schmiegelow gleefully puts it, are "all those lovely mosquitoes and blackflies and horseflies, those biting insects that we love to hate, along with a whole host of other invertebrates." The bite-sized morsels provide a feeding bonanza for breeding birds and their nestlings. Because the growing season in the North is so short, the crop of invertebrates tends to come on all at once, providing an almost limitless supply of nourishment when it is needed most. Then, when winter clamps down on the forest, the birds can take to the wing and escape to the southern states, Mexico, the Caribbean and other sun-filled getaways. Unlike most other ecosystems, in which a majority of the breeding birds are year-round residents, the birds of the boreal are mainly migrants. In fact, fully 93 percent of the landbirds in the boreal are fair-weather friends, here just long enough to catch this seasonal pulse of nutrients.

If bugs are the big attraction, they are not the whole story, Schmiegelow says. The forest's other great strength is what she calls its "intactness." It's the tree-after-tree-after-tree-after-tree-ness of the forest — its vastness and connectivity — that allows it to meet the requirements of 186 different species. If a breeding pair cannot find what they require in one place, they can fly across the lake or to the next range of hills, until they locate the resources that will make life comfortable. For instance, Cape May and bay-breasted warblers are two of a number of species that are adapted to live in the crowns of large, old spruce, particularly those that have reached an age of 80 to 120 years. Everything about these birds equips them for life at the top. For instance, the males are bright and flashy, so they can display themselves on high branches as they stake out their territories, and their lisping, high-pitched songs carry clearly up there in sky country. What's more, their staple foods are insects such as spruce budworm and tent caterpillars that erupt in the upper branches and work their way down the tree — provided that they aren't caught in the act and fed to some hungry nestling.

But the forest is not static. Old trees die of disease and blow over; they are consumed by fire. And although the forest grows back in to replace them, nothing's the same as it was before. Instead of the prickly darkness of a spruce wood, the new forest is leafy and lush, dominated by deciduous growth and with a dense understorey of shrubs. This so-called early successional forest provides ideal habitat for many species — including ovenbirds, American redstarts and yellow warblers — but it nothing to offer birds that require old-growth conifers. So the Cape Mays and bay-breasted warblers have to go looking for patches of forest that have made the transition from the early successional stage into mature coniferous stands, the only type of woodland that can meet their requirements.

It's the supreme mobility of birds — the enviable lightness of flight — that enables them to track the shifting resources of the forest. And this rule holds not only for old-growth species, but for all kinds of boreal birds, whether they are woodpeckers searching for recently burned-over forest, chickadees looking for nest holes or crossbills hunting for seed-laden spruce cones. "It takes very large areas of forest to maintain resources to support all those species, both in space and over time," Schmiegelow says. And the miracle is that, in 2004, those large areas of forest are still out there.

Sapsucker holes
Linda Anne Baker

September 4, 2003: Well, we did it — in six days, we paddled the entire 130-kilometre route from Besnard Lake to our pull-out at Missinipe and lived to tell the tale. I was so proud of my river muscles that when I got home I challenged my daughter to an arm-wrestling competition. Hey, I almost won!

Now, a month later, I am sitting in the belly of one of Air Canada's big birds, on my way from Saskatoon to Ottawa for the wind-up celebration of the Boreal Rendezvous. It's supposed to be a big folderol at the Canadian Museum of Civilization, with music by Gord Downie (of Tragically Hip fame) and his current band, the Country of Miracles.

But meanwhile, I am hurtling through a cloudless sky somewhere between Winnipeg and Thunder Bay, gazing down at the drab green fabric of the boreal forest. It looks like an immense scratchboard painting, in shades of olive, ochre and mauve, that blurs into the haze of cloud at the horizon. But what strikes me is not just the run of this glowering country: it is the scrawl of roads, like tangled skeins of string, that thread between reddish clearings. In a landscape that insists on the endless intricacies of its rocks and shorelines, the straight-line geometry of these clear cuts stands out like a sore thumb. What is all this talk about an "intact" forest?

Of all the industries that draw resources from the boreal forest, logging leaves the heaviest imprint on the land. Although Canadians have been extracting wood from their forests since the 1700s (initially to provide tall timbers

Screech owl
Linda Anne Baker

for European sailing vessels), intensive exploitation is a surprisingly recent development. In the western boreal, for example, the feller-bunchers have only been at work for the last fifteen or twenty years. But such muscle! Forestry is a major economic producer, bringing in over $30 billion in export sales each year and providing employment to hundreds of thousands of Canadians. Among them are many northern residents — perhaps one day my young friend Phil (though he'd rather join the RCMP) — people who deserve to have access to sustainable, paying employment.

Unhappily, these economic opportunities are being created at a cost to the boreal wilderness. An up-to-the-minute analysis from Global Forest Watch Canada, published just last fall, reveals that while the northern two-thirds of the boreal still meets the definition of intactness, the southernmost band of the forest has already been seriously chewed up by industrial development. (This refers not only to heavy industry but to the conversion of forest to farmland, a process that is still continuing on an unexpectedly large scale.) And alas, this worked-over tract of the forest is also highly productive for birds—the best of the best of the boreal. If boreal-forest habitat is already under assault, does this mean that the game is over for forest birds, before it had even begun?

In commissioning their report on landbirds, the twin Boreal Initiatives raised this issue with Peter Blancher. They asked for a list of species that appeared to be in trouble. The result was a catalogue of 40 unfortunate species, from great horned owls (declining at an annual rate of -0.2 percent) to rusty blackbirds (down an alarming -10.7 percent, probably as a result of shooting on winter roosts far from the northern forest). But a similar number of boreal-breeding species appear to be on the rise, birds such as Tennessee, Cape May and palm warblers. (The available data suggests they may be increasing, respectively, at rates of 0.3 percent, 0.8 percent and 27.6 percent.)

Blancher is quick to acknowledge the limitations of his "trend analysis" and admits that there is no convincing evidence for any kind of general crisis. But this is no grounds for complacency, he insists, because we really do not know what is happening out there. Although we can say which birds are present and broadly in what abundance, we do not have enough data to track their fortunes. In this opinion, he is seconded by ecologist Keith Hobson, a research scientist at the Prairie and Northern Wildlife Research Centre of the Canadian Wildlife Service in Saskatoon. "The point is not that particular species of boreal birds are increasing, staying the same or declining," Hobson insists. "The point is that we don't know what is happening to them."

Whatever the present status of birds in the boreal forest, Hobson sees trouble ahead. Over the last several years, he points out, virtually all of the merchantable timberlands in the boreal forest have been licensed for cutting — he puts the figure at 97 percent of the so-called "working forest" — and the shadow of industrial society is gradually creeping farther northward. (Although the Churchill River has so far been sacrosanct, how long will that last?) Eventually, every scrap of saleable wood in the great north woods is slated to be cut down and hauled away to the mill, to end up as toilet paper, junk mail and periodicals. This in itself is not a disaster. To the extent that logging is able to mimic the natural disturbance regime of the forest — in particular the sweep of fire — it could conceivably maintain a more-or-less natural flow of habitat and a full abundance of life.

Is this what we are doing now? Far from it, Hobson says. Cut blocks are too small and uniform; there are far too many roads, and the forest is being cut-over too often, so that it never has a chance to attain mature old growth. ("If you have less old-growth forest, you'll have fewer old-growth birds. It's not rocket science.") But could we log the forest sustainably if we chose to? Yes, Hobson contends. "It is eminently doable."

"The nice thing about forestry is that you can plan landscapes," he says. "You can say, well, by the year 2050 we want this amount of old growth on our landscape. We want this amount of burn and this amount of early successional woods. So the GIS [mapping] boys get together, plug in all the data and, boom, up comes the picture and a plan.

"My feeling is that we can log the boreal forest sustainably for all kinds of products and still keep a lot of species happy. Call me naïve, but I think it is possible."

Remarkably, here is something on which everyone seems to agree: Hobson, Schmiegelow, Blancher and the conservation lobby. It is not too late to do things differently. Ten or twenty years from now, the moment may have passed, but right now there is still a chance. "We still have incredible opportunities throughout northern Canada to maintain a lot of the forest attributes we think are important not only for birds but for many other species," Schmiegelow contends. She looks forward to the day when there will be a long-term conservation vision for the whole boreal region, complete with a network of protected areas and a standard of sustainable, ecologically based development.

"The boreal forest is mostly Crown land," Schmiegelow points out. "It belongs to all of us. The question is: do we want there to be bird song in our forest a hundred years from now?"

A version of this article was first published in *Canadian Geographic* magazine.

Great grey owl.   Linda Anne Baker

James Raffan

Love, boreal style.

Good for the Birds, Not So Good for the Birders

PETER KALM

The vast woods and uninhabited grounds between Albany [James Bay] and Canada [Southern Ontario] contain immense swarms of gnats [mosquitoes and black flies] which annoy the travellers. To be in some measure secured against these insects some besmear their face with butter or grease, for the gnats do not like to settle on greasy places. The great heat makes boots very uncomfortable; but to prevent the gnats from stinging the legs they wrap some paper around them, under the stockings. Some travellers wear caps which cover the whole face, and some have gauze over their eyes. At night they lie in tents, if they can carry any with them, and make a great fire at the entrance so that smoke will drive them away.

Dutch-born Peter Kalm travelled through the boreal by canoe in 1750.

Photos by James Raffan

The Ballad of Sluice Portage

Words and music by Candace Savage

Oh, once there were three otters,
    who lived in Besnard Lake.
They raised their heads above the waves,
    and did a double-take.
For what they saw were six canoes,
    in blue and green and red.

They shook their heads and rubbed their eyes,
    and this is what they said:

CHORUS
They said "Hello" and "How are you?"
    They said "How do you do?"
"We're guessing that you folks are from
    the Boreal Rendezvous."

The otters bowed and waved their paws;
    They said, "Please come for tea.
We've pick'rel and fresh blueberries,
    and Jackfish Jubilee."
And when the plates had all been cleared,
    the eldest otter spoke:
"Without your help our forest home,
    would all be up in smoke."

CHORUS
"This wild river is our home;
    It's really all we've got.
So when you reach your journey's end,
    please keep us in your thoughts.
To celebrate your visit here, to climax and to cap it,
We hope that you'll all take a dip,
    in our own Otter Rapids."

CHORUS
They said "Hello" and "How are you?"
    They said "How do you do?"
"We're glad to meet the people from the
    Boreal Rendezvous."

Following the footsteps of our boreal ancestors on the Churchill River trip's Rooster Portage.

Laurel Archer

Good Old Fear of Death

CATHY JONES

I was freaked out this morning about shooting whitewater. But when I actually went down the rapids I felt strong, like I could do it. I didn't feel like I was going to tip over and I felt — you know, I'm strong physically and the boys sort of gave me the feedback that they thought I was comfortable in a boat — so that part, yeah, as long as they're not sending us down Class 3 rapids, I'm in. It was doable by anybody and also fun because it wasn't dangerous. I could see where my appetite could build for doing something a bit more difficult — but you know the hitting-the-head-on-the-rock thing? The rolling-over-dead-body thing? That's where I draw the line. Very simply, I don't want to get dumped out of a boat and hit rock. Fear of death, that's what's keeping me safe today. Good old fear of death. So, as we were coming into the falls today, I got into the safety position within the canoe before we even got in the area by putting myself feet first and heading down — just to be sure.

Comedian Cathy Jones takes a break in the Berens River sunshine.

James Raffan

Waterfall Woman

BECKY MASON

Many people think of a canoe trip as nothing more than physical challenge, but I think that there are many more factors at play. Usually when we are presented with an unfamiliar situation we fall back on the tried and true coping methods that work in the city. Being on a canoe trip changes some of those methods and rules, and because of this I believe a canoe trip can challenge us to also discover new emotional benchmarks.

On our paddle down the Berens River we came to an incredible waterfall called Mikaiami Falls. After carrying the first load of gear across the portage trail, I took a minute to rest and have a look around. The raw power and beauty of the place left me awestruck. Pounding, surging water contrasted sharply with the gentle spray in the warm sunlight. Cedar waxwings darted through the glistening mist, skimming tiny bugs off of the pure waters. In the falls, I spied a place where it looked like you could sit safely and feel the power of the falls coursing over and through your body.

We finished the sweaty portage, set up our tents and decided to cool off. A few of us went to enjoy a little swim in a quiet pool halfway down the series of falls. As I floated in the pool I looked longingly at the little cataract just a stone's throw away. I decided to go and try it out. It was delightful!

To feel the river massage you in such a powerful yet relaxing way is amazing, and the blurred kaleidoscopic view from the air pocket behind the falls was beyond description. I motioned for my fellow paddlers to join me, but Anna and Cathy were worried about approaching such a powerful water source and decided to pass. At this point in the canoe trip both of them were still thinking of rushing river water as a sink-or-swim experience.

I suppose the "Mikaiami Spa," as we called it, did look dangerous to the unpracticed eye, but it was a safe place and probably an experience never to be repeated. After some explaining of river currents and morphology, as well as time spent watching the others in the falls, Anna screwed up her courage, grabbed my hand and held on tight. Cathy needed a bit more convincing, so I simply said, "There is a time for trusting and the time is now," and left the decision to her.

Emotions hung in the balance as Anna and I turned away and started to cautiously wade up to the waterfall. A few steps into the trek there was another tug as Cathy latched onto Anna's hand. So we all marched proudly on, three women united in common purpose. I was surprised to feel how much that experience strengthened our bond of friendship and trust. We got to the cascade and charged in. It felt like the daylights were being pounded out of us, but we all agreed it was the best massage we'd ever had.

James Raffan

Mikaiami Massage

ANNA BAGGIO

*Berens River trip organizer
Anna Baggio (right)
with Cathy Jones.*
James Raffan

Becky Mason and husband Reid McLachlan's passion about canoeing and exploring rivers was contagious. Their curious river spirits led us to appreciate one of the ancient secrets of Onaagaaíiiami Paawitig — the Mikaiami massage.

We arrived at Mikaiami Falls on the Berens River in northwestern Ontario on a gloriously sunny August day. Becky and Reid waded out from shore to a ledge to explore a series of pools and smaller cascades that gave way to the big, tumbling, rushing waters of Mikaiami Falls proper. Becky asked me to come out and join her in the foaming water, but my immediate reaction was — "No way!"

Becky and Reid know water. They know rapids and rocks and can paddle almost anything. I, on the other hand, am a much less experienced canoeist, and swimming is not one of my strong suits either. When I paddle rapids, I'm always a bit apprehensive about what will happen if I dump. This is what made stepping into Mikaiami Falls seem daunting.

Becky sensed my fear, but she knew something about the falls that she wanted to share and added, "Anna, you know I wouldn't ask you to do anything that wasn't safe. Trust me." And I thought, Hey, if Canada's godmother of canoeing says, "Trust me," then who was I to argue?

So off went the shirt and out came the PFD, and a few minutes later I was under the ledge letting the water tumble over my shoulders and head. It was the most amazing massage I've ever experienced — natural and wonderful. I sat in that cauldron of bubbling white water and watched the waxwings wheel and flutter, picking dinner out of the air above the rushing water. It seemed a place of tremendous power, healing and elegance. But then a sadness took hold.

Mikaiami Falls is definitely one of the most incredible spots on the Berens River. The Ojibway people from the Pikangikum area have come here for generations. Sturgeon spawn just downstream. And along with the waxwings are many other living creatures who make this stunning place in the boreal their home. But Mikaiami Falls is also the site of a proposed all-weather bridge that will connect the lands north of the Berens to services and economic possibilities in the south. I can only hope that the land-use planning agreement we're signing this summer will ensure the magic and majesty of this wonderful place.

Canoeists Becky Mason (bow) and Reid McLachlan cut a reedy corner on the Berens River below Goose Lake. James Raffan

Members of the Berens River team get a quick lesson in Ojibway names and terms from Pikangikum guides
Timothy Saggashie (Kookoog Angiigwan) and *Terry Turtle (Ogiimaa O'gwan), including pickerel (oogas) and northern lights (wawatei).* Andrea Maenza

The joy of sunshine, friendship and whitewater. Gillian McEachern (bow) and photographer Andrea Maenza collaborate to negotiate a rapid on the Berens River.

Reid McLachlan

Where Were You When the Lights Went Out?

DAVID LANG

I imagine a koan that goes something like this: "How does the light go on when the light goes out?" As with all such riddles, there is really no correct answer, only possibilities for...illumination. It came on the Berens River in the heart of the boreal forest in northwestern Ontario.

We had been living comfortably without electricity on the Berens River when, via sat-phone, news arrived of the massive power outage on August 14, 2003. If I remember correctly, all of us were busy at the time with the routine jobs that transform a campsite into a temporary home. Tents were being pitched, firewood collected, and the food for the evening meal was being prepared. Nevertheless, everything stopped when we heard the news.

My immediate reaction was to assume that there had been a terrorist attack on a major power station. The ongoing war on terrorism had left me in a constant state of unease. Others figured that a temporary overload on the power grid had been caused by overuse of air conditioning in the sweltering heat. Many of us felt the urge to make contact with family members and loved ones. All of us were drawn back to our memories of 9/11.

It was not until we returned to the town of Red Lake at the end of the trip, a day or two after the outage, that we learned the power was gradually being restored and that there had been little in the way of serious injury or loss of life as a result of the power interruption. It took me until my arrival in Winnipeg (where a trip-end celebration took place), and the subsequent exposure to the mass media, that the enormity of the event really began to sink in.

What follows is a post-trip meditation on the blackout and what it had to say to me through purposeful reflection.

While we were on the river, we were literally powerless to do anything about the situation. At the same time, we had been empowered by our experience on the canoe trip. I, for one, felt stronger and more clear-headed than I had for ages.

Lightning brightens the sky on a summer evening.
James Raffan

The trip rekindled my passion for wilderness travel. I have to admit to feeling a little bit smug when I thought about people in the city struggling through a day without computers, TVs, flush toilets, or cold drinks. I secretly hoped that it might even give some added weight to our conservation message. But there was more to it than that.

The immediate link between 8/14 and 9/11 had to do with unforeseen catastrophe and with being out of control. Nothing frightens us more. Think about how important the concept of power has been to the development of western industrial civilization! Wind power. Steam power. Hydroelectric power. Nuclear power. Automotive power. The power to tame the frontier. The power to shape our destiny.

The cabbie who took me to the Winnipeg airport had some things to say about this as well. When he learned I was from Toronto, he asked how I had coped with the power outage. I told him that it hadn't really affected me since I had been on a wilderness canoe trip. He told me that in the town where he was born, in northern India, they had blackouts all the time. Since it was a regular part of life, they had learned to deal with it by stockpiling water, cooking with gas, using bicycles and the like. He said that he enjoyed it when the power was out because all the neighbours came out onto the streets to talk.

The encounter got me thinking about just how full our language is of phrases that speak to the centrality of power in our lives. They pour into my mind improvisationally, as in a jazz tune: the power of love, the power and the glory, power play, power lunch, power nap, power to the people, flower power — feel free to add your own to the list.

While on the Berens River, we were privileged to spend time with a group of elders from the community of Pikangikum. One after another they talked about their pride in the knowledge acquired from living off the land. They seemed to gain strength from giving themselves over to a higher power. They told us that the Creator has provided for all their needs.

At the same time, I couldn't help noticing that they came to meet us on the river in boats with high-powered outboards burning fuel that was flown into the community and sold for prices roughly twice the going rate in Red Lake. The same costly fuel was being used to power the generators that provided electricity to the village. One of the elders wore a ball cap with "Native Power" embroidered in large print.

Stories in *The Globe and Mail* about the great outage of the summer of 2003 mentioned that people in Toronto and New York City, and places in between, had been delighted at the rare chance to gaze up at a starlit sky which, for once, was not obliterated by urban light spill. Stories also talked about the friendliness and kindness that people showed to one another during this time of crisis.

My special memories from our canoe trip also revolve around evenings spent with our group, telling stories around the campfire or lounging on smooth rocks, still warm from the heat of the day, and marvelling at the beauty of a night sky unpolluted by the effects of civilization. We studied the constellations and learned how to get our bearings from them. This, too, was a form of power that is as old as civilization.

Northern Lights — Paint

BECKY MASON

After last night's display, I'm burning to paint the northern lights. Can't wait to get breakfast done and pack up fast. I hope everyone is really slow packing up today so I can have lots of time to paint. I anchor our canoe to the shore, load it up and leap in, scrabbling over soft packs, rocking the canoe wildly as the water laps on hull. I cradle my painting gear in my arms until I get to the end and settle into the bottom of the canoe — home again.

Gently rocking canoe on pristine water, dripping brush scuttles over the water surface. Brush plows over paper surface thick with paint but not fast enough, wind blows — painting flies — painting flips end over end — it catches around my hand as paper tries to escape to the water. More weight secures the painting's edges.

I get into the rhythm of painting, feeling the gentle rock of the canoe as the sunlight plays across my body and paper. Almost done but slipping palette skitters across my paddle blade — catch it before it meets a watery end down down to the rocky depths. Paddle — blade — brush — water — paint — rice paper — painting goes on and on into a timeless structure.

I put it down on the bottom of the canoe, the sun dazzles and the wind whistles over the paper nestled in bow. I pick up my paint smeared paddle dip, dip, and swing my paddle and I hope the painting dries soon so I can add it to the others in our map case. My creative spirit feels rejuvenated, a Berens River memory to take home.

Lunch spot on the Berens River. Reid McLachlan

At left: **Northern Lights, Berens River,** *7"x 14" watercolour on Japanese rice paper.* Becky Mason

Lunch Spot on the Berens River, *7" x 7" watercolour on Japanese rice paper.*
Becky Mason

Of Forests and Elections

CATHY JONES

Cathy Jones, aka "Joe Crow,"
on location in the boreal forest.
Salter Street Films

I guess what I've learned through this experience in the boreal is that it is unacceptable to think that these issues are something we can leave to the left-wing protesters. I hope we are all past the point where we think that just people who eat granola are interested in the environment. I've always been the Joe Crow person who does the environmental stuff, and I used to feel slightly embarrassed, because it's always the big aggressive news that is considered more important. But I believe the environment is the most crucial issue that we have to deal with as human beings. It's front-page, top-story caliber. The vision it demands is challenging for the public because we have short-sighted leadership who are themselves lobbied to death, bombarded with the good-life hype and blinded by profit.

Being out here gives me hope because I see intact wilderness, and it is thrilling and very moving. We have it and we need to support the indigenous people who live on it, who keep it, because they are in effect our only dignified guardians. If they are not honoured and supported then we are not the great Canada we could be. When we are electing people I hope that we all will consider strongly their stand on protecting this jewel. I am extremely happy to be here participating in a situation that raises some awareness.

If you're asking me if I prefer Winners and a cappuccino from Starbucks and maybe a movie at the Cineplex Odeon or another week on the river — I'll take the river.

In a timed exposure of several minutes duration, the rotation of the Earth is marked by streaks in the northern sky.
The only star in our heavens that does not do this is, of course, Polaris, situated directly above the North Pole. Donald Standfield

Thomas King, star and writer of the Dead Dog Café and Comedy Hour, *with Laurel Archer, author and guide.*

Cathy Jones (left), star and co-writer of This Hour Has 22 Minutes, *with friends in Mikaiami Falls on the Berens River.*

Rocks and Trees and Water: A Boreal Dialogue

THOMAS KING and
CATHY JONES

Cathy Jones — So, Tom, I hear you went on one of those celebrity river trips with the Canadian Parks and Wilderness Society as part of their Boreal Rendezvous.

Thomas King (smug) — Actually, I went on two.

Jones (solicitous) — Oh, that's too bad.

King — It is?

Jones — All the really big celebrities — such as myself — only had to go on one.

King (defensive) — I'm a big celebrity.

Jones (patronizing) — Novels and radio? A couple of children's books. (beat) Wake up, Tom. All the really big celebrities are on television.

King (slightly sarcastic) — Right. (beat) So where did you go?

Jones — I went on the Berens River in northern Ontario.

King — Great. You see any wildlife?

Jones — Oh, my yes. There was this big, tall guy who started shouting and waving his arms around and making a terrible fuss.

King — On the Berens River?

Jones — No. At Pearson Airport in Toronto. (beat) He was causing such a problem they had to shoot him with a tranquilizer dart. (Jones looks at King knowingly)

King (taken aback) — You saw that?

Jones — The whole enchilada.

King (defensive) — That line was over two hours long. (beat) And it wasn't a tranquilizer dart.

(Jones look at her nails)

King (continuing) — Okay, it was a tranquilizer dart. (beat) But it was just a silly misunderstanding.

Jones — Did it hurt?

King — Yeah. A little.

Jones — So, where'd you go?

King — Well, I canoed the Churchill River in northern Saskatchewan and then I rafted down the Coal River in the Yukon.

Jones (romantic) — You know, there's nothing like the great outdoors.

King — Camping under the stars.

Jones — Cooking your meals over an open fire.

King — Breathing clean air.

Jones — Drinking water right out of the river.

King — Makes you feel alive.

(Both nod in agreement.)

Jones — Course, there was the paddling all day in the wind.

King — Oh, Yeah... And the cold feet.

Jones — Wet clothing.

King — Portages.

Jones — Rapids.

King — Dank, leech-infested bogs. (beat) You know I may never get my hosiery clean.

Jones — No cappuccino.

King — No showers

Jones — Bugs.

King — Bugs.

Jones — Bugs.

King — Bugs.

Jones — Say, did you have to do your... you know... in the woods.

King — You mean the thing with the shovel and the brown paper bags?

(They think about this for a moment and shudder.)

Jones (bright tone) — Hey, but we had a great time, right.

King — You bet.

Jones — And we learned all about the boreal forest and why it is critical to the health of our planet.

Tom (not too sure) — Oh...yeah.

(Neither one of them has a clue.)

Jones (trying to sound profound) — The boreal forest... The boreal forest... (beat) Take it, Tom.

King — Ah...well, there were rocks....and trees...and water.

Jones — Exactly. (beat) So, you want to catch a cab over to Hull and grab a latte.

King — You bet.

Jones — If you're good, I'll let you see my blisters.

King — Blisters? I'll show you blisters.

Jones — I'm not talking about the ones you get from holding onto the sides of a canoe.

King — The stupid thing was tippy.

(Jones stops and thinks for a moment.)

Jones (concerned) — Say, you don't think the people at the Canadian Parks and Wilderness Society are going to ask us to go on next year's Boreal Rendezvous.

(Both look around nervously.)

Jones — Taxi!

King — Taxi!

Jones — Taxi!

King — Taxi!

Ad lib to end

Both new to canoe-tripping CPAWS-style, Thomas King and Cathy Jones planned this little skit for the final celebration of Boreal Rendezvous in Ottawa.
King took ill and was unable to attend, so Jones carried on solo, leaving this manuscript to posterity.

Paddling below an unnamed falls on the Rivière à l'eau Claire, near the Richmond Gulf, Québec. James Raffan

LEG 4

Boreal East

The silence is a hum wrapping around everything. It is a silence made deeper by the sound of the waterfalls. This landscape is an eternal dream, or awake in a way I hardly perceive.

Writer Robert Perkins from *Against Straight Lines*,
a book describing a canoe journey across Labrador and northern Québec.

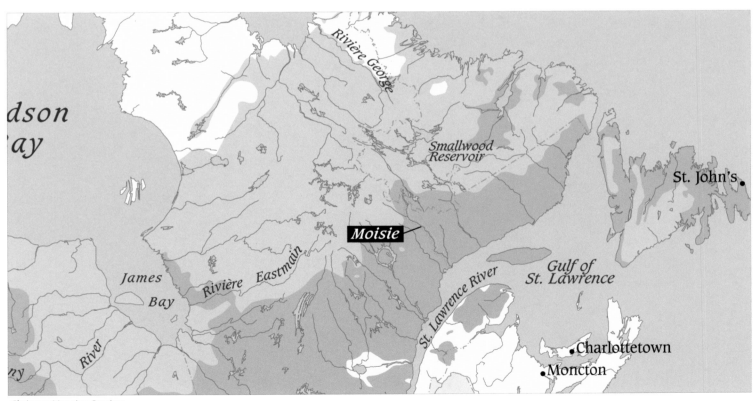

Chrismar Mapping Services

Black Spruce

Black Spruce

words + music: Ian Tamblyn

Chorus

Black spruce, black spruce heart of the northern river
Through the glass I ripple, clouds and trees I'll know
Black spruce, black spruce onwards ever deeper
Calm this restless heart, soothe this restless soul.

I am the raven high o'er the river
I am the black wings carry me home
I am the night sky deeper and deeper
So many stars always alone.

Chorus.

I am the wind sigh night through the jack pines
I am the flurry of birds on the wing
I am the silence - answer your longing
I am but a heartbeat pounding.

Chorus

I am the storm clouds building and building
I am the fury, the thunder, the light.
I am raindrops birdsong sing the morning
I am white water heard in the night.

Chorus

No more questions - all of your longing
I am these things - ask me no more
I am the whisper at the heart of your calling
Comfort your heart, slip through the door.
Chorus

July 2003, Sea Lynx Music, SOCAN

I am the night sky — deeper and deeper.   Donald Standfield

Evening on the Richmond Gulf.   James Raffan

Majestic Moisie, the Nahanni of the East. CPAWS / Michel Gauthier

Web Notes

BRIGITTE VOSS

A Tumultuous Departure

August 6 — Yesterday morning, around ten o'clock, the adventure started for eight of our team members who headed out to the Moisie River. We took off in a small Hutter-type plane and went to set up camp before the others arrived. Meanwhile, back at Lac Rapide, Richard repaired one of the rafts that had been eaten by a porcupine! Also, Tim's luggage was officially declared lost by the airline and the poor man had to return to Sept-Iles to buy new equipment! All these unplanned events led to a five-hour wait before the first half of the team could finally start our river adventure.

When we finally got going on the river, we were divided between one raft and two canoes. In one canoe was Réginald and Josée, and in the other, Tim and Jean-François. As we encountered our first Class 3 rapid, Réginald and Josée passed, while Jean-François and Tim soon found themselves in the water! Tim lost a sandal, his only pair of shoes, and to top it off, his bag was drenched because it was not properly closed. All his personal effects and his sleeping bag were wet. He then changed places with Sylvain and went on board the raft. Second rapid, second swim…both canoes were tipped over by this Class 2 rapid. Also, Jean-François and Sylvain's canoe suffered major damage. Finally, on the third Class 2 rapid, Josée and Réginald tipped over. This area was dangerous, with many rocks, but Richard mastered the situation and everyone remained safe and sound.

After all these events, the team members found a nice sand bank to set up camp and take stock, but spirits were warmed and renewed by a dinner of salmon and beef cooked in the embers. The energy within the group is wonderful.

This morning, the weather is beautiful, it is hot and the sun is shining. Today will be a quieter day, a mere forty kilometres on quieter water.

River, Laughs and Music

August 7 — All is going well for our Moisie River adventurers. After an eventful day on Monday, Tuesday went by calmly. Forty kilometres were travelled on a quiet river, in the peace of the boreal forest. Sylvain's knowledge was highly tested by questions from his fellow paddlers on biology and geomorphology.

As night fell, camp was set up next to a river named Rivière à l'Eau Dorée, and the well-deserved meal consisted of Bonanza Stew and salmon. The salmon was prepared using Josée's grandmother's recipe. It seems that the team clown is Michel, followed closely by Réginald — both crack up their friends.

After a good night's sleep, our team members headed out Wednesday morning for another easy day, only twenty kilometres to paddle on mostly flat water. But at the end of the day, we had to go around a major Class 5 rapid, le Cran Serré. Tim will remember that one. The team spirit is really incredible, everything flows between the team-mates like the water in the river. Every night Marc and Sarah bring out their guitars and sing — it's simply amazing.

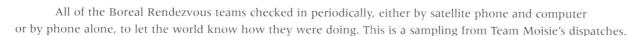

All of the Boreal Rendezvous teams checked in periodically, either by satellite phone and computer or by phone alone, to let the world know how they were doing. This is a sampling from Team Moisie's dispatches.

Teva sandal image courtesy of Trailhead, Kingston.

Notes and Sketches
from a (Wet) Moisie River Journal

TIM GRAY

DAY 4

"Ile de sable"
Rivière Moisie   T.J. GRAY

Survived the ride down Cran Serré with only a deep dunking when the raft stood vertically on a wave with all of us on board — for a moment. After, our guide, Gilles, demonstrated his kinetic acrobatic abilities by bouncing from the rafts and in short order building a circus-tent-come-kitchen using oars, a piece of nylon and a raft — all in about twenty minutes. I am exhausted from the expectation of drowning and retire to lounge in the open doorway of my tent to sketch and smoke. The river beach sand provides a matte background for the spray of dome tents, all electric colour against the misty grey-green of the soaring granite and spruce that rise from the river behind.

August 6 — No shoes and now no sandals either (they disappeared during my first plunge to the bottom of the river an hour after we got off the floatplane). I'm still in that headspace that is partly back at the office — but I can start to see glimpses of the trip-to-come in a place whose form I didn't expect. Bigger trees, higher mountains, wilder — the Nahanni of the East. We come around a corner and are greeted by the noise. We scout it out. It is not like a northern Ontario rapid, more like a British Columbia waterfall. The river drops over a slippery smooth five-metre ledge and climbs to a standing wave that collapses into the face of a granite cliff. After sorting itself out, the water reforms to charge over another five-metre fall and end in a series of seven or eight waves of two or three metres high. It becomes clear that we are going to actually raft down this thing. I hope that everyone else will chicken out so I can too. When it becomes clear that this won't happen I reconcile myself to enjoying the ride down and drowning in my fourth week of my new job.

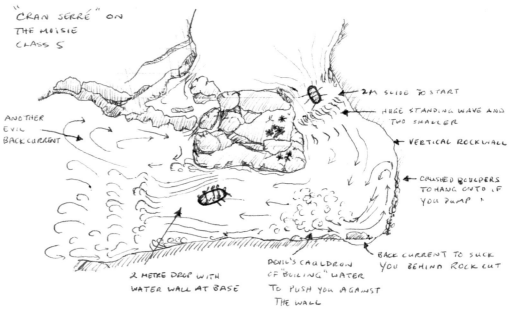

"CRAN SERRÉ" ON THE MOISIE CLASS 5

ANOTHER EVIL BACK CURRENT

2M SLIDE TO START

HUGE STANDING WAVE AND TWO SMALLER

VERTICAL ROCKWALL

CRUSHED BOULDERS TO HANG ONTO IF YOU DUMP

2 METRE DROP WITH WATER WALL AT BASE

DEVIL'S CAULDRON OF "BOILING" WATER TO PUSH YOU AGAINST THE WALL

BACK CURRENT TO SUCK YOU BEHIND ROCK CUT

Pencil sketches by Tim Gray

Two Solitudes, Not — La Moisie! | SARAH HARMER

These are some rough journal entries from the boreal, complete with my impoverished French. They barely illuminate my dramatic memories of the wild. Flying over the northern Québec mountains and peering down on the turbulent rivers destined to the mother sea. The loudness of the plane engine and the closeness of the cavern wall as we descended to the narrow river to start our water journey. The pull of the water on the oar. The look on the faces of those tossed out of canoes as they bobbed in the quick water and shot through the rocks.

Lundi — À côté de la rivière Moisie. C'est très joli. J'ai faim. Heir soir j'ai fait un rêve d'un small grey owl. I slept in a large canvas tent sandwiched in between three people. A married Innu couple — Réginald *et* Josée — *et* Brigitte. We lay on Balsam boughs, *avec un feu*, a giant fly flapping itself against the roof. The couple came to bed after me and spoke in slightly hushed tones in Innu — a rhythmic *tuktuk* staccato language. It was beautiful and soft.

Today, as last night, I am surrounded by people speaking a language I barely understand. Even surrounded by people I think this will be a solitary week. I am not homesick — yet — but I have felt small traces of it. Perhaps it would have been more engaging to partake in an English trip. Ah well, there's no getting out of it now. I should've brought a better reading book. *Tout le monde* is in conversation mode — all seeming so interesting — but I am on my own.

Tuesday — I am counting the days. I wonder what I am here to learn? This is challenging not knowing the language. I don't know how I thought I could get by. But I'm building my vocabulary:

déjà - already	*couteau* - knife
sauf - except	*plupart* - for the most part
savon (le) - soap	*faire le plein* - to fill up
quand même - all the same	*poche* - pocket
ensuite - afterwards	*court* - short
cravate - tie	

Mercredi — Things improve greatly. I will remember my feelings of homesickness and isolation, but I have made some connections — verbal and otherwise — and I am beginning to find my place. So glad I brought my guitar. The campfire jam sessions have been fabulous. Marc Déry and Florent Vollant *ont des bonnes chansons. Bonnes chanteurs. Tout le monde ici aiment rire.* Michel is a funny man. I can tell because he really gets everyone laughing. Sadly, I miss *les nuances.* We have stopped to camp for the night and, along with a few drops of rain, there is a breeze coming up to blow away *les mouches.*

I move under the tarp (*il pleut*) and a hot coffee with Baileys is served up and knocked back. The French. The Innu. I hear them laughing now as Florent comes up with Innu names for everyone. There is an inside joke on Tim, "the man with bare feet." (He lost his sandal in the fast-flowing river the first day, after the airline had lost everything else.)

Now I am by the fire, but the mosquitoes aren't intimidated by the smoke. Ah, my childish insecurity, *quand j'écoute quelqu'un d'autres* laughing and I don't understand. I think they are laughing at me. But we are not in high school and, although *les Québécois* like to tease and make fun, I think they mean well. I am really starting to enjoy them. I rafted with Gilles this afternoon, sitting like Cleopatra on the Nile. Gilles is a circus acrobat — as one might expect from a lanky Frenchman — and his English is very good.

Sarah Harmer and Marc Déry communicate musically on the shores of the Moisie River.
CPAWS / Michel Gauthier

Today is *Jeudi* and it rains. We are here for two nights next to the rapids. Last night we sat on balsam boughs (*le Sapin*) under *Florent et Réginald's tente prospecteur*. The woodstove burned warmly and everyone sat close and laughed and sang song after song after song.

Aprés les rapides! Oh la la, c'est fun! We donned our pink helmets, tightened our life vests, and after a briefing from Richard portaged to the crest of the rapids. *"On y va!" dit* Richard and we paddled head-on into the tumbling waves. *Toute le monde sont tombé dans l'eau sauf moi et* Richard. *Maintenant nous sommes fait un* sweat lodge. *Les filles* — Brige, Nat *et* Josée — are under the tarp with the hot rocks.

Vendredi — It is very wet today. *Très mouille. Il pleut beaucoup. Tout le monde est sous la tente prospecteur. Ils chantent les chansons, buvent le chocolat chaud, pensent à dîner, jouent la guitare.* All the while the water comes down around us.

Dimanche — I am now on the plane flying west to Québec City and then to Montréal. What a wonderful group of people. I am very lucky to have shared so much with them. This camping trip was truly wild. So many things to ponder. So complex and yet so simple. Communal living. Sharing everything. Being reminded that we all deserve to be here and must show gratitude for that gift by treating the Earth, and each other, well and with respect.

The "worst portage in the world" on the Rivière à l'eau Claire flowing down into the Richmond Gulf on the Québec shore of Hudson Bay. Inset: First the canoes, then the packs.

The Worst Portage in the World

JAMES RAFFAN

On days when the weather was cool and the wind kept the bugs at bay, portaging was hellishly hard work; on those days when dead insects and sweat combined to make our skin crawl and our eyes burn l'Eau Claire was a portaging challenge of legendary difficulty...

Always, when approaching a major rapid or falls we heard the sound of the menace before we saw it. As we drifted closer, this falls sounded different. At one moment we would hear the lash of pounding water; the next minute the sound would diminish to a benign rumble. The map notation sounded innocuous: simply "Portage two miles." And so began the worst portage of my life (so far).

After about an hour of humping canoes and pack loads through spruce groves, up hills, and through moss swamps and alder thickets, I was tired and in a decidedly bad humour. Portaging is a lonely business; one that leaves each body part aching and the mind barraged with a pain-induced monologue: Why did I end up with the food packs and all this loose stuff to carry? Never mind, just keep going. Why did I agree to do this anyway? Shut up! You can go farther. That burning pain at the nape of my neck. And the bugs! *Aiiiiiieeeeeee!* If only I'd studied Zen...

I emerged from a spruce and alder jungle high above the river, and all was forgotten. It took a moment or two to focus on the visual beauty, until now masked by those menacing sounds. Before me, green water was transforming into a white tumult that thundered into billows of wet mist rising out of a narrow canyon.

Off came the bug hat and shirt, and the most refreshing balm washed over my fly-stained face. I stood transfixed until the mist-spawned droplets ran down my skin. Agony and ecstasy merged; the magic of that cataract was made more powerful by the struggle to get there. It was a case of elemental extremes: first, hardship, then elation. One of the reasons for going to the wilderness is that there are no happy mediums.

We had lunch in the spray of the falls and carried on, totally refreshed. Uphill wandering on lichen-slippery slopes turned into downhill drudgery. Too tired to carry, we slid our loaded canoes over logs and rocks, down stream beds, until we became entangled in a jungle of alder growing in the bottom of our portaging valley.

Eight hours after starting, I dumped my last load on the shore and waded into the river. I knelt on a flat rock and immersed my head, opened my eyes, and began gulping. Swallow after swallow after swallow, the refreshing water penetrated and cooled. Head up, hair and beard dripping, I was struck by the simplicity of it all. At one time a person could quench a thirst in almost any stream on the continent. Now, only in pockets of wilderness like this one was it possible. Someday will there be no more "clearwater" rivers to drink from? Will anyone remember?

(Excerpted from the National Geographic Society book *America's Hidden Wilderness.*)

And at the end, an evening's rest.
James Raffan

It is the wild water that attracts many canoeists to the boreal rivers of Labrador and northern Québec. Spray skirts mandatory; snorkels optional. James Raffan

Hot Work!

A Hundred Combinations of Water and Rock

SIR WILLIAM FRANCIS BUTLER (1872)

It is difficult to find in life any event which so effectually condenses intense nervous sensation into the shortest possible space of time as does the work of shooting, or running, an immense rapid. There is no toil, no heart breaking labour about it, but as much coolness, dexterity, and skill as man can throw into the work of hand, eye, and head; knowledge of when to strike and how to do it; knowledge of water and rock, and of the one hundred combinations which rock and water can assume — for these two things, rock and water, taken in the abstract, fail as completely to convey any idea of the fierce embracing in the throes of a rapid as the fire burning quietly in a drawing-room fireplace fails to convey the idea of a house wrapped and sheeted in flames.

Boreal Rendezvous participants rafting the Moisie. CPAWS

Notes from a George River Journal

GEOFFREY PEAKE

August 2 — From the air, this country takes on a whole new perspective. From ground level, the lakes and trees seem to be a hopeless jumble. From 4,000 feet, however, these pieces come together much like a jigsaw puzzle. Patterns in the rock and water emerge, clearly tracing the cracks and gouges made by mile-thick glaciers thousands of years ago. Caribou trails cross and braid across the landscape like unwoven threads. And in all directions this checkerboard of rock and water stretches to the horizon.

August 4 — Tonight we are another twenty kilometres down the river, camped beside an impressive gorge. My thoughts today were focused on Dillon Wallace and Clifford Easton and their tortuous journey down this river in much different circumstances than ours.

When Mina Hubbard and Dillon Wallace, each with their respective expeditions down the George, set out, they literally camped across from each other off on the Naskapi River. For some reason, Wallace decided to have his group follow the arduous Native route which climbed rather steeply out of the Naskapi River Valley, following a chain of lakes on the plateau, to meet up again with the Naskapi just before Lake Michikamau. Why he did this is not clear. He claimed to be taking a more exploratory route rather than "hiding in the river valley," as he felt Mina Hubbard's party did. Perhaps the idea of travelling together with her group up the long climb to Michikamau was just too unpleasant. Whatever the reason, by going via Seal Lake he guaranteed that he would not be the first to George River Post.

Losing over a month in that journey, they did not reach Lake Resolution until September 20. A combination of illness and inability to find the outlet from the lake, they wasted six days in a vain search for the river. When they finally did find the river, the weather turned savage as the first grip of winter laid hold to the land. For two days they were struck by a foul gale that dropped several inches of snow on the ground. Finally, on September 29, disaster struck.

Easton wrote in his journal, "Everything covered with ice; rocks along shore and water in bay. Water froze as it fell, both of us in the boat and outfit covered with frozen spray." Entering a short, steep rapid, the canoe struck broadside on a rock and capsized. Their gear was not lashed in and much of it was lost, including their rifles, axes, and pots and pans. They floundered about in the icy water in a vain attempt to recover their gear before it all disappeared. When they came ashore, Wallace knew he had to light a fire or they both would perish. Easton writes, "No feeling in any part of my body and fast losing consciousness. Managed to crawl and hobble through rapid to shore." With no wood on shore, Wallace and Easton paddled across the small bay with their hands (they had lost their paddles). Wallace's trembling hands were barely able to light the matches. By luck, the fire lit and they were brought back slowly from brink of death.

Today, as we passed that same rapid (one that we ran without mishap) I tried to imagine Wallace and Easton on the bank, fear and desperation in their eyes, praying that the fire would light. We had brought a large magnet with us, and Tom trolled the rapids while I steered the canoe in a vain attempt to hook onto one of their cherished rifles that lay, ninety-two years later, somewhere beneath our boats. After an hour, we moved on. We had our own rapids to run, and the thought of them always creates a sense of anxiety until the day is over.

Approaching the George River in Ungava, Québec by floatplane. Seductive beauty. Michael Peake

Just South of Lac Lacasse

PETER BREWSTER

Sitting here in the bush with a $4,000 laptop on my knee and waves pounding the beach — and caribou no doubt grazing over the ridge — is a new hat that will take a few days to wear easily. Never mind the solar panel trickling power into the sat-phone battery and the digital Nikon lying on a sleeping bag like it, too, belongs. So what's for supper? *That* I understand.

Peter Brewster is a member of the Toronto-based Hideaway Canoe Club, which in recent years has reported on trips in real time on the internet, in much the same way as Boreal Rendezvous participants kept in touch during the summer of 2003. This e-journal snippet is from the archived log of a journey that took place in August 1997.

Waves on a crescent beach in George River country, northern Québec.
Michael Peake

Visible and invisible diversity in the boreal. Even the pool of proteolytic enzymes inside the insect-eating pitcher plant are a moist home for three species of mosquitoes that have adapted to use the harsh environment as a nursery for their larvae while all other unsuspecting critters are digested. Linda Anne Baker

Parts of the southern boreal, including this campsite in Gros Morne National Park in Newfoundland, are accessible not by canoe but by footpath and bicycle. James Raffan

To Feel Blessed

CARRIE McGOWN AND MARTHA MORTSON

So what? There's power and challenge and demand in this question "So what?' So we paddled 9,000 kilometres across Canada — covering waterways in our canoe from Saint John, New Brunswick, to Tuktoyaktuk, Northwest Territories, most of the journey taking place in the boreal forest — so what!? What does this journey mean? To us? To others? To the land? What's the point? This is what we now know:

Priorities are different and better when our To Do reads: notice the birds, identify clouds, paddle.

When everything we need to live comfortably and happily for five months fits in a canoe, why do we own more?

Without a mirror to examine the shape and appearance of our bodies, we judge ourselves by accomplishment rather than appearance and at the end of the day are more appreciative of our strength for having carried us further along.

So often on our journey it was cold — some days our feet alternated between cold and painfully cold. And we don't like the cold. But we decided it's good to be cold. It's part of what being out there is about. At home, when it's cold, it's easy to be a lump on a couch. But out there, on trip, we're forced to keep going, forced to experience unpleasant circumstances. Cold makes us feel alive, tough, capable, strong and helps teach us to appreciate what we might otherwise take for granted.

We must know our natural heritage. When encountering animals and birds we recognize, there is great excitement, much like unexpectedly crossing paths with a friend in large city.

Entering dozens of communities by canoe, we wondered about our reception. Being paddlers and women gives us an "unthreatening" presence; still, people could have chosen to ignore our passing. Instead we were embraced. How do we make friends out of strangers if we don't arrive in a canoe?

Windbound, looking out on the water, we knew a picture would only capture turbulent water, yet none of drama and emotion of what it is really like out there in a canoe. There are times when words are worth a thousand pictures.

The "north bug" bites as surely as do her mosquitoes and black flies — don't go north unless willing to be powerfully and irrevocably bitten!

Martha Mortson (left) and Carrie McGown in Tuktoyaktuk in 2001, at the end of their three-summer, 9,000-kilometre canoe journey to raise awareness about the beauty and value of the boreal wilderness. Many Rivers

Surprise encounter around a boreal bend — for the paddlers and for the cow moose and calf.   Marten Berkman

Sometimes we would feel badly telling people that we were paddling across Canada because they would immediately start downplaying their own trips and experiences. Why compare journeys?

So often people asked, "Aren't you scared...out there in the wilderness...all alone...two girls...all those wild animals?" Our most frightening experience happened along the Saint Lawrence while camped in a city park. At 3 A.M. a truck screeched towards our tent, people hopped out, cursing and screaming, shook the tent violently and then ran away. There are more crazy people in urban settings than there are crazy bears in the wilderness. We rarely felt fear in the forest.

Why do we feel pressed to account for not paddling? "There's thunderheads moving in, we should stop" or "Listen to that wind, we should stay." Must circumstances be threatening before we permit ourselves to rest?

We set off in 1999 on our Many Waters expedition to discover what it means to be Canadian through the land and its people. Our answer? To be Canadian is to be blessed with a generous land and generous people. We are changed because of our journey.

So what about you? Will you get outside? Will you choose to allow the forest to change you? Will you care for others and for the land?

For three summers, Martha Mortson and Carrie McGown paddled from St. John to Tuktoyaktuk, on an odyssey they called "Many Waters." Remarkable about this extended journey was not that two determined and able women successfully met every challenge the trip could offer, but that they stopped repeatedly along the way, taking time to give more than 200 presentations to schools and interested groups about what they saw and learned along the way, particularly what they learned about the beauty, power and value of the boreal forest. In many respects, Many Waters was a prototype for Boreal Rendezvous, and as such, Martha and Carrie were invited to add their voices to *Rendezvous with the Wild*.

St. John River Valley, where the "Many Waters" expedition began. Linda Anne Baker

A Sunset in New Brunswick

WILLIAM T.
GRIFFIN

I wish I could paint the picture I gazed upon last night,
Just as the day was ending in a soft and fading light.
A rainy day was over, a new moon hung in the west
Just where the storm-clouds lifted and the sun had gone to rest.

The river in the valley and the wooded islands green,
The silver on the water and the wash of golden sheen
On the forests in the background and the hillside far away —
In a picture, all were blended at the ending of the day.

In the sky, the colour changing as the day turned into night
Where a single diamond twinkled, a lone star growing bright.
Another day was ended, another night was born.
From the records of creation another leaf was torn.

But time goes on unending and the sun will rise again,
The great Creator only has the power to explain
The mysteries of the universe, while man can only guess
How many million years ago, or billions more or less,
The plans for last night's sunset were completed in detail,
God, He knows the answer...you and I must fail.

From *You're on the Miramichi.* William T. Griffin (1881–1974) spent his life in
the New Brunswick woods as father, woodsman, trapper and guide.

James Raffan

Berens River participants examine the map and plan the next day's travel. James Raffan

Rendezvous with the Wild | The Journey Continues

ANNE JANSSEN

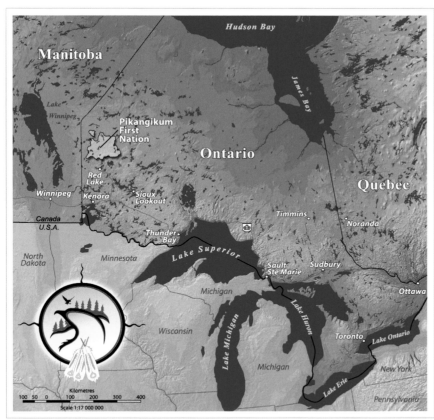

Marcel Morin

In 2001, the Canadian Parks and Wilderness Society (CPAWS) launched a program to protect Canada's boreal forests as one of the last wild and intact places left on Earth. Throughout the boreal, CPAWS chapters are sitting at land-use planning tables, engaging in discussions with industry players and working closely with First Nations in their communities.

The starting point for the CPAWS Boreal Program is different from earlier forest conservation campaigns for several reasons: overall thinking has shifted; we have the luxury of being proactive rather than reactive; we have a society ready to do things differently; conservation organizations are more collaborative; and, not least, we have industries that are moving away from business-as-usual processes and exploring new, more forest-friendly modes of operation.

During 2003, two exciting agreements were signed that show just how differently business in the boreal is being conducted. Nationally, a bold action plan for the conservation of Canada's boreal forest, called the Boreal Forest Conservation Framework, was developed and endorsed by eleven leading organizations, including conservation groups, forest industry partners and First Nations. As well, during Boreal Rendezvous, a historic regional cooperation agreement was signed between the Whitefeather Forest Management Corporation and the Partnership for Public Lands that set new standards of cooperation both for the protection of the forest's natural and cultural values and for sustainable development to meet the needs of the Pikangikum people in northwestern Ontario.

CPAWS was pleased to play a leadership role in these efforts and was grateful to be working with such excellent people as the chiefs and council of Pikangikum First Nation as well as Cathy Wilkinson of the Canadian Boreal Initiative, who coordinated the development of the Conservation Framework. As the journey continues, their stories follow.

The Geography of Hope

CATHY WILKINSON

The Athabasca River is the longest and among the most storied rivers in Alberta. It rushes out of the mountain glaciers near Jasper, but by the time it curls around the forested flatlands of Wood Buffalo National Park, its urgency is gone. Eddies barely lap the sandy shoals. Above them, ravens call lazily. On this languid part of the river in a canoe was an excellent place to begin to understand the contrast between natural beauty and the threats that are beginning to overwhelm the boreal forest through which it flows.

Today, only seventeen percent of Alberta's forests are not logged, developed or crisscrossed by roads. Most of this development has occurred within the past ten years. This remarkable pace of transformation was not so much deliberate as it was simply unplanned. With no orchestration or coordination, a pulp mill has popped up here and a mining operation has opened there; suddenly Alberta's boreal forest is like other wilderness places around the world, in that it finds itself subject to a multitude of diverse pressures.

Alberta's boreal is still an important home for wildlife species such as the lynx and snowshoe hare, and a nesting ground for thousands of migratory birds and waterfowl, but their habitat has been dramatically altered in many areas. And while many local groups, First Nations, and leading resource companies are committed to maintaining the integrity of these forests, in many places they are playing catch-up.

There is a portent here, in Alberta, of what's to come in the rest of the boreal if we fail to redefine our relationship with the region. The fragmented woodlands of Alberta and elsewhere across the country call out for a national vision to guide development. Fortunately, much of the forest survives in its natural state and, at this juncture in our history, we have an opportunity to make its future different than its past.

My job constantly sends me back and forth between the cities of southern Canada — where eighty percent of Canadians live — and the boreal forest. Again and again, this trip takes me across a sort of boundary that separates the people who want to know why we should conserve the boreal and the people north of them to whom the question is unimaginable. It's not a geographic boundary; it's a psychological one. Traversing this line has altered my thinking.

Linda Anne Baker

Illustrations by Bill Mason

When I am in cities, the question of why we should conserve the boreal doesn't seem at all strange. Nor is the answer difficult: we need the boreal for the kind of environmental maintenance that even southern cities can't be without — the quality of our air, water and climate depends on it. But when I visit the boreal region — when I'm surrounded by a vast sea of forest or when I'm among the people who live in it — the question seems almost absurd, while the answer becomes both more difficult to articulate and, at the same time, more quietly and completely satisfying.

The boreal forest covers half the country, but most Canadians have yet to get there. They haven't been on the Athabasca River at dusk when silhouetted spruce make a serrated edge along a wide Alberta sky. They haven't seen the lichens of Labrador, as colourful and as strange as tropical coral. They've never paddled through mournful loon serenades over northern Saskatchewan lakes. They have only a vague sense of the majesty and worth of these places.

Linda Anne Baker

A quarter of the world's original forest is found in the boreal. It is one of the largest remaining intact forest ecosystems on the planet. It is home to healthy populations of bears, wolves and caribou. A third of the continent's bird life nests there. Many of our First Nations communities rely on it in the same way they have for millennia. The boreal is, in short, a rare original in our modern world of trammeled wildernesses.

Working together on behalf of the boreal forest is among the last opportunities we will ever have to develop and manage a large-scale ecosystem in an effective and sustainable way. It is a one-time-only chance to avoid the mistakes of the past, the mistakes we've unthinkingly visited upon so many other natural wonders in the world.

In a 1960 essay, American writer Wallace Stegner described wilderness as the "geography of hope." Without wilderness, men and women become numb to who they are. Humans as a wild species risk their own domestication. "Something will have gone out of us as people," he writes, "if we ever let the remaining wilderness be destroyed." The boreal forest is Canada's geography of hope. It is an opportunity to sustain something whose absence is keenly felt in other parts of the planet (not least in Stegner's United States, where less than five percent of the country is designated wilderness). Canadians are characterized by our relationship with the wilderness. "Survival" in the wild is our unifying Canadian theme, writes author Margaret Atwood: Nature is not for us to subdue but to be ventured into as a test of endurance. "Our stories," writes Atwood, "are likely to be tales not of those who made it but of those who made it back."

Even if we never get there, the country's northern woods are part of our make-up. Something will have gone out of us as people if we ever let the remaining wilderness be destroyed.

Linda Anne Baker

I have spent a lot of time in communities across the boreal region, drinking tea with people and talking about its future. I always come away with a renewed sense that the character of the boreal has much to do with those who live there, those who pick berries and who hunt caribou. There is a closeness they share with their environment. The place and the people make a seamless impression.

On the final day of our Athabasca river trip, Archie Waquan, Chief of the Mikisew Cree, and Archie Cyprien, Chief of the Athabasca Chipewyan and Grand Chief of Treaty 8, landed a floatplane in our midst to lay out a wine-and-cheese lunch for us on a mid-river sandbar. The gesture underscored the notion that this place is home to these chiefs and to the others who live here. Anyone who has ever been a guest in such circumstances will understand what I mean: the sense of someone's home has to do with their familiarity, comfort and ease in a place. Nothing else. It is not self-conscious. It is effortless. Boreal residents are at home in these landscapes; it is no less and no more remarkable than that.

I am convinced that we need a national vision to manage and sustain Canada's boreal forest — not because we want to stop time or to build a fence around the boreal to save it from change, but because we have a rare opportunity to change our relationship with this ecosystem so that it continues to function forever. This isn't about how much is left; we need to take the opposite approach. Instead of calculating the minimum amount of forest that can be left intact to accommodate development, we need to ask how much can we afford to take out of the system and still safeguard it as a source of abundant natural species, vegetation and fresh water.

The Boreal Forest Conservation Framework is a national vision to sustain the ecological and cultural integrity of Canada's boreal forest region. It was unveiled by the Canadian Boreal Initiative and our partners in December 2003 after extensive consultations with First Nations, leading resource companies and conservation groups. The key to it is establishing comprehensive land-use planning for the entire boreal forest region.

The recommendations reflect the unique character of the boreal. For instance, the ecological processes of the boreal forest depend on regular, large-scale disturbances. Fire is a key regenerator of the forest. It needs a vast sweep to kindle the natural cycles of the region. Insect infestations also have a role, and their periodic population surges feed birds and other keystone species in the ecosystem. Water is another force shaping the region, and it too requires uninterrupted space to cycle through the boreal's millions of lakes, rivers and ponds. By their nature, these features of the forest need both adequate room to move and adequate connections to one another. The framework has been designed to recognize these scale-dependent requirements.

At the same time, we also need to make room for economic development — both for the inhabitants of the boreal region and for southerners who have long relied on its resources. That's why the framework allows for the full spectrum of human uses and sensible development. It is intended to recognize the need for viable commercial enterprise in the region that will contribute to a sustainable economy for area communities. Ultimately, governments will have to ensure that comprehensive land-use planning is in place to minimize the haphazard fragmentation of the forest while ensuring the best possible conservation standards. The framework is not about arresting development; it is about sustaining it.

I did not grow up in the boreal forest. My childhood was spent on the beaches of Prince Edward Island. My sense of nature was formed by the Atlantic. Later, I would understand the parallels between the ocean and the boreal forest. Both possess an apparent limitlessness that can make us believe that our mortal efforts will always be insignificant by comparison. That conclusion is wrong. If nothing else, our northern cod stocks have shown us that. The impact of uncoordinated development that is slowly moving into the boreal is another good illustration.

My trip on the Athabasca was a timely reminder of why I believe so strongly that Canada needs a national vision to manage and sustain our boreal forest. This amazing set of interconnected ecosystems is important to our environment and our health. It's important to our climate. It's important to the culture and the livelihood of the peoples who live there, and it's important as an indelible part of our national psyche.

Linda Anne Baker

The river is still their road. To get to the end of the dusty two-lane south to Red Lake, Ontario, residents of the village of Pikangikum must first travel by boat, in summer, up the Berens River and past this spectacular rapid. Aluminum runabouts and outboard motors are portaged with the help of wheeled carts on a little inclined railway that travels on a boardwalk on the west side of the river. Andrea Maenza

Doing Business Differently

JAMES RAFFAN

Below the 51st Parallel in northwestern Ontario, leases to cut timber have historically been written with scant community consultation. Above the so-called cut line, the Pikangikum First Nation is at the forefront of the Anishinabe–Aski Nations' effort to do things differently — to create forest jobs only after identifying and setting aside areas that shouldn't be logged for cultural or ecological reasons.

Last August, in the remote Ojibway community of Pikangikum, some 100 kilometres northwest of Red Lake, Ontario, the Boreal Rendezvous Berens River team witnessed the signing of a historic agreement between the band and a consortium of environmental groups to create a comprehensive land-use plan for a 1.3-million-hectare parcel of Canada's boreal known as the Whitefeather Forest.

Chief Paddy Peters and elders welcomed the paddlers to a feast of moose meat and wild rice in the Pikangikum Hotel and afterward spoke optimistically about the future. "The Creator gave us this land," explained councillor Oliver Hill. "Everything we need is in this land. We want to look after it. But we want to do it our way. That is why we're signing this agreement." Pikangikum says its consensus-building partnership with the Canadian Parks and Wilderness Society (CPAWS), the Federation of Ontario Naturalists and the World Wildlife Fund is rooted in cross-cultural respect and shared values for the protection of lands that are the heritage of all humanity. It adds that it is committed to achieving economic self-sufficiency through commercial forestry of its ancestral land, but in a way that preserves biodiversity and protects important habitat for woodland caribou and wolverines.

"To help do that," says Alex Peters, president of the Whitefeather Forest Management Corporation, "we're very pleased to link with the Partnership for Public Lands [consortium]."

Anna Baggio, a member of the Berens River team and CPAWS signatory to the agreement, adds, "This partnership signals a new way of doing business in the boreal."

Pikangikum Chief Paddy Peters (right) and CPAWS–Wildlands League Director, Northern Boreal Program, Anna Baggio signing the historic land-use planning agreement.
Andrea Maenza

The Sun is Beginning to Shine Again

CHIEF PADDY PETERS

I'm choosing to speak in Ojibway, my native tongue. We are one of the strongest communities in the area. Only about one percent of people from here leave town. One of the strongest things about our community is our language.

Our elders say that the land sustains us. By signing this agreement we are welcoming help from outside to look after our land. This is a largely inaccessible place. At times we have eighty percent unemployment in the community. And, especially lately, we haven't had much positive press. This community land-use planning has been going on for the past five years. And by signing this agreement we're hoping things will change.

But let's do it our way. Let's do it the way we want to. Let's be in charge. A lot of times the land is stripped and it dies, and the animals die with it. We don't want our animals to die. We don't want our birds to die. We want to keep our land the way the Creator made it. But yet we want to be in charge to do it our way. We want jobs as well. And this planning process may achieve all that.

This is a historic day for our community. I believe the sun is beginning to shine on this community. And I believe it will shine for many more months to come.

THE WHITEFEATHER FOREST INITIATIVE: ECONOMIC OPPORTUNITIES AND RESOURCE STEWARDSHIP

A PARTNERSHIP FRAMEWORK

LETTER OF AGREEMENT

BETWEEN: **Pikangikum First Nation**
AND: **The Partnership for Public Lands (CPAWS–Wildlands League, Federation of Ontario Naturalists, World Wildlife Fund Canada)**

PREAMBLE

The people of Pikangikum First Nation are the keepers of a land-based indigenous way of life that has been passed on to them from their ancestors. Their culture is a vital part of the cultural diversity of humanity. Through their indigenous way of life they have always cherished the diversity of all living things and non-living things on their land.

Pikangikum First Nation people have developed the Whitefeather Forest Initiative as a community economic renewal and resource stewardship initiative to provide livelihood opportunities for their youth in keeping with their cultural teachings and values. The initiative is being guided by the Elders of Pikangikum. The vision of Pikangikum people for the Whitefeather Forest Initiative is based on acknowledgment that the Creator placed them on ancestral lands, where they have lived since time immemorial. It is also based on an acknowledgment that they are to take care of their lands as a sacred trust given by the Creator. Their vision for the Whitefeather Forest Initiative is also one of partnerships rooted in cross-cultural respect and shared values for the care and protection of their ancestral lands, which they know are part of the heritage of all of humanity.

Pikangikum First Nation and the Partnership for Public Lands share a common vision to protect and take care of the land and resources in the Traditional Territories of the Pikangikum First Nation that will form the basis for the Whitefeather Forest Initiative. This shared vision respects the teachings and wisdom of Pikangikum Elders that supports the care and protection of the diversity of life on the land. This shared vision supports dialogue and working together on the basis of respect and in a manner that will bring together the best of different knowledge traditions. It is on this basis that we are able to enter into our agreement set out below.

Map courtesy Marcel Morin

PARTNERSHIP PRINCIPLES

In this agreement, Pikangikum First Nation and the Partnership for Public Lands are establishing a relationship of cooperation and partnership in relation to the Whitefeather Forest Initiative. Both partners acknowledge that this partnership is based on mutual respect for the views and aspirations of each party and recognize that our organizations have limited means but that we work together where possible to create success in mutual endeavours.

The Whitefeather Forest Initiative is centered on Community-Based Land Use Planning, an approach that has now been adopted as policy under Ontario's Northern Boreal Initiative (http://204.40.253.254/envregistry/06410ep.htm). (Title: Northern Boreal Initiative - Community-based Land Use Planning Approach). It is the position of both Pikangikum and the Partnership for Public Lands that:

1. Community-Based Land Use Planning will be completed prior to any development activities, including the establishment of protected areas and the commencement of commercial forestry within the Whitefeather Forest Planning Area.
2. Community-Based Land Use Planning should guide the identification and development of resource-based opportunities, including protected areas, and infrastructure development in the Whitefeather Forest Planning Area.

It is the desire of both parties to establish a strong partnership for the Whitefeather Forest Initiative based on our complementary strengths and abilities. We agree that:

1. The Whitefeather Forest Planning Area and adjacent areas are "... a geographic area that is a cultural landscape, modified, influenced and given special meaning," by the Pikangikum First Nation People;[1]
2. The outcomes of the Whitefeather Forest Initiative will maintain the ability of the Pikangikum people to pursue cultural and livelihood activities on the land;
3. A primary goal of the Whitefeather Forest Initiative will be to conserve biodiversity and protect viable populations of Woodland Caribou and Wolverine and their habitats as part of the overall strategy in which the Partnership for Public Lands and Pikangikum will cooperate to establish and manage an interconnected system of protected areas within the Whitefeather Forest Planning Area.
4. We will work cooperatively with the Province of Ontario to establish the Whitefeather Forest Initiative, guided by the Elders of Pikangikum First Nation and centered on the Indigenous Knowledge tradition, environmental values and perspectives, and customary indigenous stewardship values and practices of Pikangikum people and harmonized with broader-scale ecological considerations and provincial responsibilities of Ontario;
5. The economic benefits of Whitefeather Forest Initiative should flow primarily to the Pikangikum people.

ᑭᑭᑐᐃᐧᓇᓂ ᐅᒋ ᐊᐱ ᑲᑭᐃᐧᓯᓂᓇᓂᐊᐧᑭᐸᓂ ᐃᐃᒪ ᐱᑲᒋᑲᒥᑭ ᐊᑎᑌᒥᓂᑭᓯᓯ, ᐣᓴᐁ ᓀᓭᓭᓵᐅ

ᐊᓴᒥᓇ ᑭᑕᐧᒥ ᐃᐧᓭᑲᓯᑫ ᑭᓯᓯ

ᓂᐃᐧᐃᔑᑭᘁᐧ ᐃᑎᔑᑭᘁᐧᐃᐧᓂ ᐊᓂᔑᓇᐯᒧᐃᐧᓂ ᐃᑎᔑᒥᓂᑯᐃᐧᓂ ᒥᐅᐁᐧ ᐯᔑᑭ ᐃᐣᑯᓂᑲᓂ ᑫᔦᐱ ᑲᐃᔑᑭᘁᐧᐊᐧᒋ ᐅᑎᔑᑭᘁᐧᐃᐧᓂᐊᐧ ᐯᔑᑭ ᑕᓯᐱᐊᐧᐱᑯᓯ ᐁᑕ ᐃᔑᑭᑫᒋᑲᑌ ᐁᐅᒋᒪᒐᐊᐧᒋᐯᔑᑭ ᑫᑯᓂ ᒪᐊᐧᒋ ᐁᒪᐣᑲᐊᐧᑌᑭ ᐅᐅᒪ ᐃᐣᑯᓂᑲᓂᑭ ᐃᐃᐁᐧᓂᑕᔑ ᐅᑎᔑᑭᘁᐧᐃᐧᓂᐊᐧ

ᐃᑭᒋᐊᓂᔑᓇᐯᒥᓇᓂᑭ ᐃᑭᑐᐊᐧᑭ ᐅᐅᐁᐧ ᐃᑕᑭᒥᓇᓂ ᑫᔦᐱ ᐁᐱᒪᒋᐃᑯᔦᑭ ᐊᐱ ᐅᔑᐱᐊᒪᓂᐅᐅᐁᐧ ᐊᓭᑕᒪᑎᐃᐧᓂ ᐃᐸᑭᓇᑭ ᑯᑕᑭ ᐸᑲᓂ ᐊᐃᐧᔦᑭ ᐊᑲᐧᒋᑭ ᑲᐊᔦᐊᐧᒋ ᒋᐱᐃᐧᒋᐃᓇᑲᐧ ᐊᓂᓂᑫᔑᑲᓇᐊᐧᐸᑕᒪᑭ ᑭᑕᑭᒥᓇᓂ ᐊᐱᒋ ᒥᓴ ᐅᐅᐁᐧ ᑲᐸᐸᒥᒋᑲᑌᓯᓄᑭ ᐊᔦᐃᐧᓂ ᒎᓴᑭ ᑲᐃᐧᓂ ᐊᔦᒪᑲᓯᓄᓇᓂ ᐊᓄᑭᐃᐧᓇᓂ ᓂᓴᐧᓯᒥᑕᓇ ᑕᓯᐱᐊᐧᐱᑯᓯ ᐃᔑᑭᑫᒋᑲᑌ ᐁᐊᔦᓯᓄᑭ ᐊᓄᑭᐃᐧᓂ ᐃᐃᒪ ᐃᐣᑯᓂᑲᓂᑭ ᔑᑲᐧ ᒚᒥᑕᑫ ᑲᐃᐧᓂ ᒥᓇᐧᒋᒧᐃᐧᓂᑭ ᐃᑎᐸᑭᒥᑯᓯᒥᓂ ᐃᐃᒪ ᑎᐸᑭᒨᒪᓯᓇᐃᑲᓂᑭ ᐅᐅᐁᐧ ᐃᐣᑯᓂᑲᓂᐃᐧᐊᐧᑭᐃᐧᐊᐧᐸᒋᒋᑫᐃᐧᐅᐧᔑᑕᐃᐧᒋᑫᐃᐧᓂ ᐊᓴ ᓇᓄᔦᑭ ᐱᐅᒋᑕᔑᑭᑲᑌ ᔑᑲᐧᑕᔑ ᐅᔑᐱᐊᒪᓂ ᐅᐅᐁᐧ ᐃᐧᒋᐃᐧᓀᑕᒨᒥᐁᐧᐃᐧᓂ ᐃᐸᑯᓭᑕᒥᓂ ᒋᐊᒋᓭᑭ

ᑕᑲᑕᔑ ᑐᑕᑕ ᑭᓇᐃᐧᑎ ᑲᐃᐧᑐᑕᒪᑭ ᑕᑲ ᑐᑕᑕ ᐊᓂᓂ ᑲᐃᐧᐃᔑᑐᔦᑭ ᑕᑲ ᑭᓇᐃᐧᑎ ᑭᑲᐅᑭᒪᑲᑕᒥᓂ ᒎᓴᑭ ᐅᐅ ᐊᑭ ᒪᓴᐣᑯᓂᑲᑌ ᔑᑲᐧᔑ ᒥᐃ ᐁᓂᔑᓂᐳᒪᑲᑭ ᔑᑲᐧᔑ ᐊᔦᐊᐃᐧᓴᑭ ᒋᓂᔑᐊᐧᓇᑎᓯᐊᐧᒋ ᑲᐃᐧᓂ ᐱᓅᔑᓴᑭ ᐃᑕᑕᐁᐧᓂᒪᓯᐊᐧᓇᓂᑭ ᒋᓂᔑᐊᐧᓇᑎᓯᐊᐧᒋ ᐅᐅᐁᐧᑕᔑ ᓂᐃᐧᐃᔑᑲᓇᐊᐧᐸᑕᒥᓂ ᐃᑕᑭᒥᓇᓂ ᐊᓂᓂ ᒪᓂᑐ ᑲᔑᐊᑕᐁᐧᑕᑭᐸᓂ ᒋᐃᔑᑲᓇᐊᐧᐸᒋᑲᑌᓂᑭ

ᑲᐁᑕᔑ ᑕᑲ ᓂᐃᐧᐅᑭᒪᑲᑕᒥᓂ ᐊᓂᓂ ᑫᓂᐊᐃᔑᓭᑭ ᐊᓄᑭᐃᐧᓇᓂ ᐃᑕᑕᐁᐧᑕᒥᓂ ᑲᐁ ᔑᑲᐧᔑ ᐅᐅᐁᐧ ᐅᔑᑕᐃᐧᓂᑭ ᑭᑲᑲᐣᑭᒋᑫᒥᓂ ᒋᑌᐱᓇᒪᑭ ᐅᓄᑲᑭᓇ

ᒥᐃᐸᔦᔑ ᐁᐃᔑᓭᑭ ᐅᐅᑎᓄ ᐃᔑᒋᑫᐃᐧᓂ ᐅᐅᒪ ᐃᐣᑯᓂᑲᓂᑭ ᐃᑎᔑᑌᐯᐧᑕᓂ ᑭᓯᓯ ᐊᓴ ᐁᓭᑲᓯᑫᒋ ᐅᐅᒪ ᐃᐣᑯᓂᑲᓂᑭ ᔑᑲᐧ ᐃᑌᐯᐧᑕᓂ ᒋᓭᑲᓯᑫᒋ ᑭᓯᓯ ᑫᔦᐱ ᐁᐧᑎ ᓂᑲᓂ ᑭᐳᓭᑲᑕᐃᐧᓂᓂᒥ ᐃᐃᒪ ᐱᑲᒋᑲᒥᑭ ᑭᓇᐊᐧ ᐱᐃᐧᑌᑭ

Translation of English into Ojibway syllabic orthography was made possible by facilitator Andrew Chapeski and translator Randolph Suggashie.

CHARLIE PETERS

(Chief's father)

I'm still working. I'm the ex-chief, ex-council member. I brought the first telephone system to this community. One of the first jobs I had was cutting the line to bring in that system. Before that, I used to trap in the Goose Lake area. As a young man I didn't have knowledge of these issues [respecting forest conservation]. Back then, I didn't know the resource potential of this land. Now I know that there are lots of resources, lots of potential. A long time ago, we didn't understand why the white men were getting money to cut down trees. The more I study that, the more I see that there is money on the land. Everywhere I look now, I am starting to see money. I didn't really understand that when I was growing up.

It is fitting that this signing is occurring on the flag of our community. Its blue, green and yellow colours stand for water, land and sky. It symbolizes our deal with the Queen, which is to go on as long as the river will flow, as long as the sun will shine.

ᑕᑕᐱ ᐊᒪᐤᐸᐠ ᓂ ᑫᐅᐅᑉᐸᒧᐠᐊ ᑫᐅᐅᑕᐱᐁᐧᐄᐊᓂ ᓂ ᓄᑕᕋ ᐊᑭᐯᓇᐤ ᑭᑉᒋᐅᔕᐧᑕᐧᓄ ᐅᐅᑦ ᐊᓐᑫᐤᑲᐱ ᓄᑕᕋ ᐊᑐᓄᐤ ᐸᐸᕈᓇᓗᐤ ᐊᑭᐊᓅᐸᕀ ᐁᐸᓗᐱᐧᐅᐱᔐᓄ ᐅᒋ ᓌᐤ ᑭᑉᒋᐅᔕᐧᑕᐧᓄ ᑕᐧᑲᑎᐢ ᑭᐊᐅᑉᔭᕀ ᑕᑕᑉᐊᐧᐊᓂ ᐊᐸᕀᓂᐊᐧᐊᓇᓇᐁ ᐁᐟ ᓄᑭᐱᐊᑭᐱ ᔑᐱᐧᐱ ᐊᐸᕛᐧᐃᔕᐠ ᐁᐟ ᐟᔑᑉᐸᔕᐧᐊᐸᓇ ᐃᐧᐠᐢ ᐸᐅᔕᑕᐧᐱᐧᐊᑕᕀ ᓇᐧᑕᐤ ᐁ ᐊᐸᐅᔭᐠᑉᑕᕀ ᐅᑖᐸᐱᑎᐢ ᑲᐧᐊᓂ ᐊᐸᐅᓄᐣᐟᐸᐧᐊᓂᕐ ᐁᐱᕐᐧᓇᐅᑉ ᐊᐠ ᑲᐅᐟᑕᓄᔑᑭ ᕐᑖᑉ ᐊᐊᐧ ᐊᐸᐠ ᐅᑖᕀ ᐊᐟᐢ ᓄᓇᕐᑕᐊᓇ ᐊᐧᐱ ᐧᐸᑕᓄᐟᐱ ᕐᐊᕀ ᐊᐧᐧᐊᐟᓇ ᑲ ᑕᐢ ᐸᓇᓄᐱᐟᐧᐊᕐ ᐊᐧᐊᑖᕋ ᐊᐱ ᐊᐟᓄᕐᐟᑕᐊᓇ ᓄᔕ ᐧᐟᐱᕐ ᐊᐊᐧ ᐊᐸᐠ ᕐᐱᐧ ᐧᐊᐊᐧᐱᔕᐧ ᓇᐧᕐᐧᑕᐧᐸ ᓄᔕ ᑲᐊᓄ ᐧᐧᐊᐧᓄ ᐊᐱᐅᕐᑕᐁᐧᐊᓇᕀ ᓌᐤ ᐅᑖᕀ ᐅᐟᔑᕐᐸᔕᐠᓄ ᐧᕀᑖᕐᕀᐠ ᐊᐊᕀ

ᐊᐸᐱᐧᐅᒪᓇᐱ ᐅᐧᐱᐟ ᐊᔓᐊᐸᓇ ᐅᓄᐊᔕᐤ ᓄᑲᐱ ᔕᑉᒐ ᐅᐊᐧ ᕐᑕᐢ ᐅᓄ ᑲᐊᓇᔕᐱᑭᓄ ᕐᒐᐊᐟᐸ ᐧᐊᐧᓇᔕᐱᐧᐅᑉᓄ ᐅᐱ ᔕᐠ ᐊᐧᐊᐧᕀᕐ ᕐᑕᐧᔕᐊ ᐧᔑᐱᐸᐧᐠᔭᐱᐧᐅᑉᓄ ᐅᐟ ᐊᐊᐧᐤ ᑲᐊᐧᐁᑉᕐᐧᐄᓗᕐᑎᐧᐅᓄ ᐧᕀᐅᑉᐧᓌᐧ ᕐᑕᐢᐊ ᓅᐟᐱ ᐊᐧᐅᐟᓄ ᐅᐊᐧᐊᔑ ᐊᔕᐊᐧᐟᐱ ᕀᐱ ᔕᐧᐧᐅᐟᓄ ᕐᐧᐸᔑᕐᐊᐧᕀ ᔕᐸᐸᕐ ᔕᐧᐧᐧᓄ ᐅᑉᑉ

Charlie Peters signed text in Cree syllabics

PARTNERSHIP PLANNED ACTIONS

Pikangikum and the Partnership for Public Lands agree to pursue a series of actions to help realize the Whitefeather Forest Initiative in a timely fashion:

Pre Tenure Period — Planning and Building Capacity

1. Pikangikum and the Partnership for Public Lands will cooperate with Ontario so that Community-Based Land Use Planning within the Whitefeather Forest Initiative area is completed. This land-use plan will include a protected areas network and areas that will be identified for inclusion in a forest-management tenure. This will be completed by 2005.

2. Areas identified as suitable for forestry through the outcome of the land-use planning process will become the areas where Pikangikum will seek forestry tenure in 2006.

3. Pikangikum and the Partnership for Public Lands will cooperate with the Ontario government to ensure a process to apply the provision of the *Environmental Assessment Act* for the Whitefeather Forest Initiative and achieve coverage by 2006. This is to be done in a manner that addresses the particular community-based needs and vision of Pikangikum First Nation for the Initiative and the ecological circumstances of an intact northern boreal forest ecosystem.

4. The Partnership for Public Lands endorses the efforts of Pikangikum to secure funding to undertake Community-Based Land Use Planning and associated tasks for the Whitefeather Forest Initiative. These tasks will include skills development, business planning, and infrastructure development.

5. The Partnership for Public Lands endorses the protected areas Accord between Pikangikum, Little Grand Rapids, Pauingassi, Bloodvein and Poplar River First Nations.

6. The Partnership for Public Lands will cooperate with Pikangikum and the Ontario government to develop an agreement for a forest management regulatory system for the Whitefeather Forest to achieve the economic, social and environmental objectives of Pikangikum.

7. The Partnership for Public Lands and Pikangikum First Nation will work in cooperation to ensure that the forest management system developed for the Whitefeather Forest meets or exceeds the requirements of the Forest Stewardship Council certification program.

8. The Partnership for Public Lands and the Pikangikum people will participate in workshops at Pikangikum to examine future protected areas stewardship arrangements in the Northern Boreal Forest, starting with a cross-cultural dialogue on current protected areas management practices in Northwestern Ontario and how a new cross-cultural approach could result in culturally appropriate and sustainable protected areas management in the Whitefeather Forest.

Post Tenure Period — Protected Areas Stewardship and Establishing Economic Opportunities

9. The Partnership for Public Lands endorses the objective of Pikangikum to ensure that primary economic benefits from resource extraction and protected areas in the Whitefeather Forest area go to the Pikangikum people.

10. The Partnership for Public Lands will participate (where feasible) in the Whitefeather Forest Research Cooperative in its efforts to engage the Ontario Ministry of Natural Resources, the Great Lakes Forest Research Centre and, forest industry and university partners and to carry out research supporting forestry and other livelihood pursuits in the Whitefeather Forest.

Nothing in this agreement shall prejudice in any manner or any way any of the Treaty and Aboriginal Rights of the citizens of Pikangikum First Nation or the Treaty and Aboriginal Rights of any other First Native person.

The parties signing this Agreement represent that they are familiar with, and agree to the terms and conditions set forth in this agreement and that they are duly authorized to sign the Agreement and agree and intend to be bound by the Agreement.

In signing this Letter of Agreement, we solemnly seek continued gifts of good guidance and strength from the Creator in our efforts ot work together on developing our partnerships in the Whitefeather Forest Initiative.

Signed this _15_ day of _August_ at Pikangikum First Nation.

For Pikangikum First Nation

_____
Chief

_____
Deputy Chief

_____
Councilor

_____
Councilor

_____
Councilor

_____
Councilor

_____
Councilor

_____
Councilor

_____
Councilor

_____
Councilor

Signed this _15_ day of _August_ at Pikangikum First Nation.

On behalf of the Partnership for Public Lands

_____
Anna Baggio
Director, Northern Boreal Program,
CPAWS-Wildlands League

_____
Gregor Beck
Director, Conservation and Science,
Federation of Ontario Naturalists

_____
Anne Bell
Acting Executive Director, CPAWS-Wildlands League

_____
Steven Price
Director North America Programs, World Wildlife Fund Canada

SOLOMON TURTLE

The river is still the same as when the Creator created it long ago. I don't know when the Creator made this river, but it is our job to look after it. I appreciate how far you have come to support us.

ᒥ ᐸᓯᑳᓂ ᐁᐊᐸᒷᐯᑊ ᑲᐁ ᓂᐱ ᐊᐱ ᒪᐅ ᑲᐅᔡᐦᐱ ᐱᐱᔭ ᐅᑕᐱ ᑲᐃᐧᐸ ᐊᐱ᙮ᐸᑭᑐᓇ ᐊᐅᐧᐊᐱ ᑲᐅᔡᐦᐱ ᓴᐳᔡ ᐱᑲᐧᔡᐦᐱᒷᐦᑭ ᐸᐧᔡᐸ ᒷᐸᓇᐧᐸᐸᐳ ᓂᐣᐅᐧᓂ ᐊᐦ ᐊᐳᐨᒷᐊᐸ ᐁᐊᐧᐸᐃᒷᐸᐠ

OLIVER HILL

I am in love with this land. This land raised me. I was born on the land. I am in love with this land. The land is my mother, in a manner of speaking. The Creator gave us this land. Everything we need is in this land, the trees and the water.

Our elders said that everything you see around you is money. There was a prophecy that one day our children would survive with a writing stick. It was also prophesied that one day our land would be a checkerboard. Our elders foretold this.

We want to look after this land. That's why we have been doing community land-based planning for the past five years. We have said "no" many times. But now we want to be a part of what's happening. We want to do it our way. We want to be in charge. That's why we're signing this agreement. That's what I wanted to tell you.

ᓂᔡᒐᐧᓂ ᐅᐅ ᐊᐱ, ᐅᐅᐧ᙮ ᐊᐱ ᐊᐱᐊᐧᐃᐊᐱᐊᒐᐧᓂ ᐊᐱᐊᐨᐸᐧᐸᐸᐸ ᐅᐅᓓ ᐊᐱᐱ ᓂᔡᒐᐧᓂ ᐅᐅ ᐊᐱ, ᐅᐅ ᐊᐱ ᒪᐊᐧᐸᐧᐣ ᓂᐳᐸ, ᒪᐅ ᐱᐱᒪᐧᐸᐨ ᐅᐅ ᐊᐧᐸᐧᐸ ᐳᐊᐸ ᐊᑐᐧ ᐸᐊᐧᒷᐧᐸᐣ ᐊᐧᔡᐳᐸᐧ ᐊᐊᒪ ᐊᐱᐱ, ᐊᐱ ᒪᐣᐦᑭᐱ ᒪᐊ ᓂᐱ

ᐊᐱᒪᐊᐧᐸᑊᐁᐧᐸᐅᐧᐱ ᐸᐊᐧᐨᐅᐧᐸ᙮ᐸᐸᐊ ᐧᐧᐸ ᐸᐧᐦᐸᒷᐳ ᐊᐸᐧᐣ ᐧᐊᐣ ᐳᐸᐱ ᐃᐳᐸ ᐸᒷᐅᐧᐸ ᐊᐳᐸᐊᒷᐱᐸᐸᐨ ᐧᐸᐧᐸᐱᒷᐸᐧᐸ᙮ ᐳᐸᐃᐸᐸᐨᐸ ᓂᐅᐸᐨᐣᐸᐸᑊ ᓴᐸ ᒪᐊᐧᐊᐸᒷᐸᐨᐊᐱ ᐅᐅᐧ᙮ ᐊᐱ ᓂᐊᐧᐸᐸᐨᐊᐧᐸᑊ ᒷᐸᑭᐱ ᐸᐊᐧᑐᐧᐸᑊ ᓂᐊᐧᐨᐸᐸ ᓂᐊᐱ ᓂᐊᐧᐸᐅᐸᐸᒷᐸᐧ ᒷᐧᐸ᙮ ᐁᐅᐧᐸᐨᐊᒷᐊᐧᐸᓇᐧᐸ ᒪᐧᐸ᙮ ᐧᐨᐸᐧᒷᐸᐊᐸᐸᑊ

The River We Live On

GIDEON PETERS

Pikangikum elder Gideon Peters describing a medicinal root from the boreal. James Raffan

This agreement is the culmination of the land-use planning we have been working on. This coming together of people is a historic event. This is the beginning of a good thing. The land has always been here. I've always lived on the land. I've never left this land to pursue an education. I'm proud to say in my own Ojibway language that we love this land.

Our forefathers foretold that the land around here would one day become like the tiles on this floor. Who gave them this knowledge, this ability to foresee? I'm very excited in the times we're living in to see these things coming to pass. If I were able to speak English, I would have lost my culture, my language.

The river we live on is called the Big River. There are many things that the river is keeping, like sturgeon and other fish. There are many people who depend on this river. It not only sustains us but sustains many other communities as well.

The Creator gave us this land. That is why I love this land. But we were given this land to share. The Creator says that those who are humble will inherit this land. That's why I'm happy to have our guests here this afternoon. I want you to stand with us to protect this river. That is my last word.

ᐁᐁᐧ ᐊᐧᐸᐋᐧᒐᐠᑐᐋᐧᐊᐧᐸᐳᓅᐋᐧᓂᐊᓂ ᐊᓅᑲᐧᐊᓅ ᐊᐧᐊᓱᐧᐸᒃᐊᐧᑭᐊᐧᐸᐠ ᐊᐧᐸᑭᓐ ᐊᐊᓇᓪ ᐊᐧᑭᐊᐧᑲᐠᒐᑭᑐᐠᒐᑕᐊᐧᓯᐋᐧ ᐊᐧᐸ ᐊᐧᐊᑭᐊᐧᓯ ᑲᐧᐸᐧᑲᓕᑭ ᐁᐁᐧᑕᐧᐢ ᑲᓪᓇᓱᓅᐠᑭᐊᐧᐧᑭ ᐯ ᐋᐧᐸᑕᐧᓯᐧᐧᐸᒃ ᐧᐸᓯᐧᐧᐊᐧᓯᐧᐸᐧᑎ ᐊᓇᐧᐸ ᒐᓂ ᐋᐧᑭᓅ ᐊᐧᓂᓯᐧᐳ ᓕᒐ ᐋᐧᒐᐧᐃᐧᑭ ᑭᑎᑲᐧᐃᐧᐸ

ᐊᓂᒐᐧᓇᐧᓯᐸᓐ ᑭᐳᐊᐧᑲᐧᑕᐧᐊᐧᑭ ᐁᐁᐧᐊ ᐊᐧᐸᐧ ᐊᐧᐊᐧᐊᐧᓯ ᑭᐳᓂᓯᐧᐠ ᒐᐋᐧᐸᒃᐧᐊᓅᓅ ᒐᐋᐧᑫ ᐸᐧ ᒐᒐᓅ ᑲᐧᐊᐧᓂᐧᑲᓕᐧᐣ

ᐁᐧᑯ ᐊᐧᐊᐧᐃᐧᐸ ᑭᐊᐧᒐᒐᑯ ᐊᓂᐧᓇᒃᐧᐸᑭ ᓂᐊᐧᐋᐧᐊ ᐁᐧ ᐊᐧᑭ ᐅᑲᐧᓅᑕᐧᓄ ᑕᐧᑭᑭ ᐊᓪ ᓯᐧᐣ ᑭᑭᐠ ᐊᐧᑕᐸ

ᓕᒐᑯ ᐊᓇᒐᐧᑕᐧᓄ ᐁᐁᐧᓅ ᐊᐧᐸ ᒐ ᐊᐧᓯᐧᐳᐳᐸᑭ ᐊᓅᐧᐊᐧᒐᓅ ᐁᐁᐧ ᐊᐧᑭ ᒐᐧᓅᐊᐧᓇᐊᓅᓅᐸ ᓕᒐ ᐊᐧᑭ ᑲᐧᑲᐧᑕᐧᐊᐧᑭᓅ ᒐᐧᐊᐧᑭ ᐊᐧ ᐊᐧᑭ ᓕᐊᐧᐧᓅᒐᓅᐊ ᑲᐧᐊᓯᐧᑭ ᐳᐧ ᑭᑲ ᑭᑲᐧᐊᐧᑭᑲᐧᐸ ᓇᒐᐧᓯᒐᓕᐠ ᓅᐃᐧ ᑲᐧᐊᓅ ᐊᐧᐃᐧᐊᐧ ᐊᐧᓄᒐᐠ ᑲᐧᐸᓅᑭᑐ

With CPAWS–Wildlands League staff member Chris Henschel intently looking on, Pikangikum elder Norman Quill explains the husbandry and harvest of wild rice during celebrations that accompanied the signing of the land-use agreement. Andrea Maenza

NORMAN QUILL (Chief's father-in-law)

Y ou have to respect the land. A lot of our younger generation don't know how to respect the land. We cannot take for granted the beautiful day we have today. And we have to look beyond today to the future, to the days of our grandchildren. I'm telling our people that we must protect this land. We must stand together to protect these lands.

ᐃᑭᑎᐃᓄᑕ ᐅᐅᐧ ᐊᑭ ᓂᐱᐊᐧᐃ ᐅᕁᑫᐧᐊ ᑲᐃᓄ ᐅᑭᕁᑕᓇ ᐊᓄ ᐃᐊᓇᕆ ᕿᕐᑭᐃᓄᑫᑭ ᐅᐅᐧᓄ ᐊᑭᓄ ᑲᐃᓄ
ᒣᕐᑕᑕᕐᓇᕆᕁᑭᐸᓂ ᐅᐅᐧ ᑫᑊᓇᕐᑫᑊ ᓅᒣ ᓴᑫᐧ ᓄᑲᓇᕁᐊ ᕆᐃᓇᐱᐧᑭᓇ ᐁᑎ ᐊᓗ ᐅᕁᑫᕁᒣᐧᕐ ᐊᑭ ᐅᕐᕿᓇᐅᕁ
ᓄᐃᕐᑕᑕᐃᑊ ᐊᓄᓴᓇᐧᑭ ᕁᑫᕁᐸᓇᐧᕐᑕᕁᑊ ᐅᐅᐧ ᐊᑭ ᒣᓗᓗᐃᕁᐸᕆᕐᕁ ᕿᕿᐸᓇᐧᕐᑕᕁᑊ ᐅᐅᐧ ᐊᑭ

CPAWS / Malcolm Edwards

CATHY JONES

Those elders are usually men of few words — and today they shared so much with us and were so generous. I thought it was an incredible way to end. It could have been so difficult to leave that trip. Meeting these people made the difference, and I wish them all the success in the world with this Whitefeather Initiative. There will be many conflicting scenarios for them. Obviously they need to make a living. It is an ambitious thing to undertake the sane development of an area so that animal habitats and the environment will be taken into consideration while at the same time people are clamouring for jobs so that they will not be destitute. It's very tricky. A lot of things need to co-exist and maybe they'll be a success story. I hope that this agreement with the Partnership for Public Lands will give the people of Pikangikum a better chance. It's a precious piece of history that went down here today.

Logs on the Mattagami River in northwestern Ontario begin their journey to mills and southern markets hungry for pulp, paper, plywood, hardwood and softwood lumber, joists, fibreboard, strandboard and linerboard. The most valuable forest product by sales is wood pulp produced by mills in Dryden, Thunder Bay, Red Rock, Terrace Bay and Marathon. We must move toward a balance between environment and commodity. James Raffan

Forest Connections and Disconnections

HUGH STEWART

The winter solstice is near. When I wake, the house is dark and chilly. I go downstairs and stoke the woodstove with well-seasoned birch and maple cut two winters ago. I go outside to untie the family dog comfortably curled in his wooden doghouse. The morning ritual moves on to putting birdseed on the wooden deck railing. The grosbeaks, bluejays and redpolls mysteriously appear en masse from nearby trees. They have been waiting, unseen but observant. I sit at the maple kitchen table and have my breakfast while watching my bird friends eat theirs. Behind them is a 180-degree panorama of trees, hills and valleys. It is a view that excites me as much today as when I first saw it eighteen years ago. It is only 7:30 A.M. and I have already interacted a number of times on different planes with my immediate forest and with the larger forest that I do not see.

Soon I go down the hill to my workshop, where the stove is also hungry for fuel. It has always seemed pleasurable and appropriate for us to heat with wood, since our activity is building wood-canvas canoes. It has been a busy fall in the shop. Much of it Dave and I have spent milling rough cedar into hundreds of ribs, and what seems like miles of sheeting, for our winter's canoes. To many the work might seem dull and routine, but for us it is a wonderful way to pass the fall. We work outside on a big deck close to the trees. We see the leaves turning, feel the crisp, frosty mornings and relish the short, warm midday. We see and feel the days getting shorter and darker.

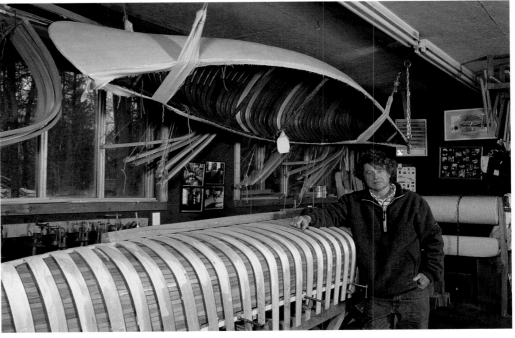

Author Hugh Stewart in his shop near Wakefield, Quebec.
Tim Wickens

As late fall turns to early winter there is a perverse, unspoken reluctance to finally admit that we must hunker down and work inside from now until late March.

During the morning, Rod is sheeting a 16-foot Prospector. This canoe is one of a number we will build this winter for a major customer, Camp Temagami. Their canoes are paddled in northern Ontario and Québec each summer by young people learning the skills of wilderness canoe travel. The experience nurtures self-confidence, increases physical strength and teaches the benefits of working in a closely knit group. The list of other customers this year is varied. A 14-foot lightweight Muskrat is for a friend's mother, in her late sixties, to paddle at the cottage. A 17-foot Prospector is for a man who wants to introduce his young family to canoe-tripping. They are all going to be used by people travelling in the forest, having experiences they will cherish.

Many times I have tried to explain to people why we prefer wooden canoes when embarking on summer travels in the boreal and beyond. I seek an experience that is in contrast to the industrial society in which I live. Thus, a canoe whose origin is in the petrochemical industry or the tires of the auto industry is of no interest. I do not want my means of travel to stand in the way of the experience I seek. It is easier to feel close to the landscape in a canoe that can be made from the forest around me.

Much of my morning is spent grading and sorting the batch of cedar ribs and sheeting that we finished yesterday. Earlier in the fall we made a number of trips to our wood suppliers in the Renfrew area. Will told us that this year he milled about 100,000 board feet of cedar, out of which there were around 3,000 board feet of clear, knot-free lumber suitable for our needs. Even though we start with the highest quality wood, over half is wastage: shavings, sawdust, cut-offs, compression wood. Like many specialized woodworking operations, we require a lot of trees .

At midday I take a five-kilometre drive to the village for regular stops at the post office, bank, hardware store, grocery store and café. Along one stretch of highway is a guardrail bolted to 8 x 8-inch posts. A few years ago, when road expansion was done, I watched these posts being installed. They are eight feet long, most of which is buried. I stop and walk along the guardrail. I pace off three chains; there are thirty-four posts. These posts are pressure treated, which suggests either jack pine or red pine. Given how big these species of tree grow, the optimum yield might be, on average, four posts per tree. I know that there are fifty chains to a kilometre, so each kilometre of guardrail bolted to wooden posts has required approximately 140 trees. For about one kilometre of my trip I am on the main highway running north-south up the Gatineau River valley. I encounter two logging trucks, one carrying spruce sawlogs and one carrying hardwood pulp. I have often wondered how many trucks would be seen if you sat at the intersection for a day. Most days I see logging trucks.

Very soon I come down the hill into the village. The outdoor rink is now up, with sheets of plywood forming the "boards," reinforced by 4 x 4-inch posts. Plywood is an everyday commodity, but we can easily ignore the vast industrial structure that is required to harvest trees and manufacture it. The rink is lit with lights on telephone poles. Poles, another everyday forest product, but one that is specialized and requires its own mini-industry. Poles cannot taper too quickly and must be long and straight, cannot have big branches, must be able to be pressure-treated or coated and be somewhat rot resistant. Only a few species meet the requirements; red pine and jack pine being the most appropriate and available.

As I turn at the main corner in the village, I can see our major tourist attraction, a wooden covered bridge across the Gatineau River. This bridge was rebuilt a few years ago to replace the original bridge, which had been destroyed by fire in the 1980s. It is good to know that the main structural material came from 550 recycled Douglas fir beams. These had an earlier life as boom logs during the lumber drives on the Gatineau and other nearby rivers. The bridge is 288 feet long, and when we consider material for decking, siding, roof trusses and strapping, approximately 150,000 board feet of lumber were required. Using conversions from Will's sawmill, our tourist attraction has used a minimum of 350 good-sized white pine, spruce and fir trees.

I stop at the local store for milk and a copy of *The Globe and Mail*. Oops, newsprint, another commodity requiring forest resources and a large industrial infrastructure. This fall the store was totally rebuilt. Wood was used everywhere:

framing materials, pine shelving and railings inside and siding outside. The community seems pleased with the new look. Wood gives the store a warmth and helps make it a pleasing place to be. Across the road, Jim runs a bed-and-breakfast in a grand home originally built by the first doctor in the village. It is called "Les Trois Érables," as it sits in the shade of three huge silver maples. Maple syrup, a local forest product, is a featured menu item. This fall the large front porch was rebuilt: spruce for framing materials, pine for flooring and finishing trim, and cedar shingles on the front. More wood, more trees, more jobs.

Leaving the village, I follow another logging truck of pulpwood up the hill on the bypass. My tally of guardrails for the trip is about three kilometres, which, for its posts, required 420 trees. After lunch we bend the ribs for an 18-foot Prospector. It is always exciting and thought-provoking to build this model. The form we use was built in the mid-1920s and was purchased from the Chestnut Canoe Company when it ceased operation in 1979. It is made of wood battens an inch square fixed to hardwood stations. We did some repairs in 1983, replacing a few of the battens. The rest is original wood. Durability! Don, who makes canoes in Fredericton, was sales manager at Chestnut for many years. With his help we have figured that over a thousand canoes have been made on this form. Many of the canoes were for industrial users: the Geological Survey of Canada, various provincial Forestry Services, prospectors, surveyors, timber cruisers. In Sept-Isles, in the early 1980s, at the end of a Labrador canoe trip, we encountered a man who told us he had surveyed much of the route for the Québec North Shore & Labrador Railway in the 1940s in 18-foot Prospectors. All the canoes we build off this form now are for recreational users. Different era, different uses, but the same travel skills to traverse the landscape.

As the work day draws to a close, I am thinking of these many contrasting forest uses. Whether it is our cedar boards, the plywood for the rink, the poles for the lights, the 2 x 4s and 2 x 6s for the store, or the newsprint for our morning paper, we all expect these forest products to be available locally, in good quantity, and at reasonable prices. We often forget the huge industrial installations, investment and the vast network of skilled foresters, technicians, loggers, truckers, mechanics, sawyers, engineers, millwrights, machine operators, graders, managers, businessmen, distributors, and salespeople who make it possible. This network provides many jobs that feed many families. At the same time we also expect huge amounts of our forest to be pristine and untrammeled when we embark on recreational travels. Many feel the quality of their wilderness trip has been diminished if any signs of logging or the forest industry are encountered.

Technological innovations purport to have made us more interconnected than ever before. Information is accessed and facts are moved instantly on the Internet. People at computer screens are told that what they are doing is completely "interactive." And yet, when I think of the boreal forest, all forests, I sense that there is more disconnection than ever before. Society's dependence on the forest for crucial products and employment is much less clearly understood than it was seventy-five or a hundred years ago. Many who seek a winter or summer sojourn in the forest forget that they are also forest product consumers. The forest is seen as a place we travel to for a wilderness experience: camping, canoeing, hunting or fishing. This experience is sought and treasured because it brings personal renewal, physical challenges, an appreciation of the power of the natural forces and is spiritually uplifting. It is also fun, most of the time, and inspires many of us to paint, photograph or write about the landscapes we've seen and

adventures we have had. Some go so far as to try and link the experience to a national identity.

There are other disturbing disconnects to ponder. Industrial and recreational demands on our forests are increasing, and the need for skilled and innovative forest management is more critical than ever. But, too often forest management practices get short-circuited by the need to achieve plant and mill quotas. The technologies to manufacture forest products or process logs into lumber can change dramatically with engineering breakthroughs. Bigger, faster, quicker can be achieved, but an equivalent increase in the supply of raw forest products is not so easy. There are limits to how fast we can make trees grow.

I wonder if the public is fully aware of what has happened to the management of our forests in the last decade. Staff in Natural Resource ministries across the country have been dramatically reduced. Many of these reductions have been at the technician level, the caretakers and policemen of the forests. These are the people who traditionally have monitored the forest industries, estimated timber volumes, and worked on regeneration projects. Now, much of this work has been handed over to forest companies. We have lost many of the leg men and women who have gathered data for foresters and entomologists studying forest diseases and forest pests. These are the people who enforce hunting and fishing regulations and gather the data on wildlife populations and health for the wildlife and fishery biologists. Unwisely, forest research facilities have been reduced and some closed. Trees are like people. They are complex biological entities subject to various diseases and stress from many sources. There is still much to be learned about how trees work and how to keep them healthy, just as is the case with humans.

People are excited about government cutbacks, lower taxes and the removal of government regulations, but do we really want the industries that use the public forests to be their own monitors? Do we really want governments to abdicate their responsibility to look after our public lands? In recent years I have travelled in two wilderness parks in Ontario, Wabakimi and Lady Evelyn–Smoothwater, which do not have master plans that the public can see, do not have any regulations (that I could find) and, most importantly, do not have staff in the field or an official presence on the land. The bureaucratic infrastructure required to look after our public lands has been shredded. Creating more parks is not the key to saving our forests. Green blobs on maps accomplish little. The public must be convinced of the need for much more natural resource management and research, not less. Governments must be convinced of the need to allocate the money and undertake the work.

It is now dusk and I bring a few armloads of firewood into the house. I stoke the woodstove, sit down and think about the day. Are my roles as wilderness traveller and wood consumer incompatible? I do not think so. Rather, they make me feel very connected to the forest. I am ready to relax in the warmth from the burning wood, drink a cup of tea and read the paper.

Liz Mitchell

The Carpenter

PATRICK LANE

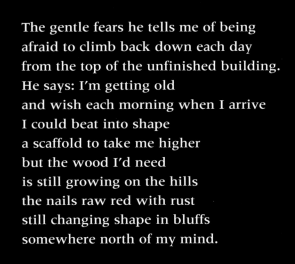

The gentle fears he tells me of being
afraid to climb back down each day
from the top of the unfinished building.
He says: I'm getting old
and wish each morning when I arrive
I could beat into shape
a scaffold to take me higher
but the wood I'd need
is still growing on the hills
the nails raw red with rust
still changing shape in bluffs
somewhere north of my mind.

I've hung over this city like a bird
and seen it change from shacks to towers.
It's not that I'm afraid
but sometimes when I'm alone up here
and know I can't get higher
I think I'll just walk off the edge
and either fall or fly

and then he laughs
so that his plumb-bob goes awry
and single strokes the spikes in to the joists
pushing the floor another level higher
like a hawk who every year adds levels to his nest
until he's risen above the tree he builds on
and alone lifts off into the wind
beating his wings like nails into the sky.

Marten Berkman

SUZA' TSETSO

What this forest means to me is history and power. It means a lot of strength and power and energy, just from being in this sacred place. What this river journey has meant to me is that there's hope for the wildlife that's in this area. There's hope too for the people who will come here in the future to enjoy this beautiful, sacred place — to be part of the mountains, the water, the trees and the land. This is heaven.

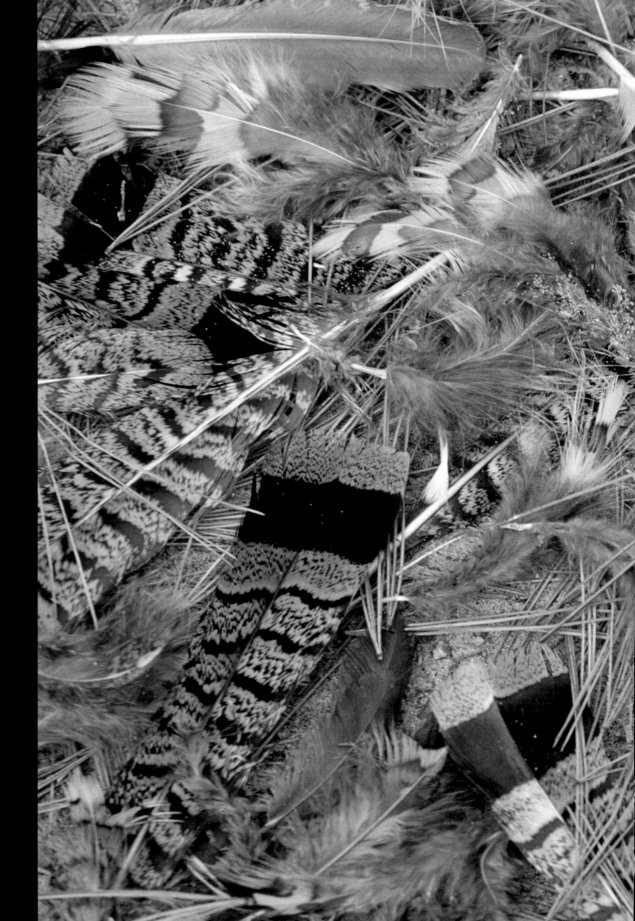

GEORGE B. STRANG

There is medicine in this land. There is money in this land. There's certainly going to be a balance there. Our planning must create employment for our people, our community, but at the same time the land must be preserved in a way that will also preserve the animals and the birds on this land. We cannot destroy the rivers. We cannot destroy the waters. There must be a perfect balance. In order for us to build a working relationship, we need to set aside areas for medicine and areas for money.

Beneath a steadfast white pine, ruffed grouse becomes fox, feathers become soil, nutrients become tree — the essential cycle of life, death, birth and rebirth in the boreal.
Donald Standfield

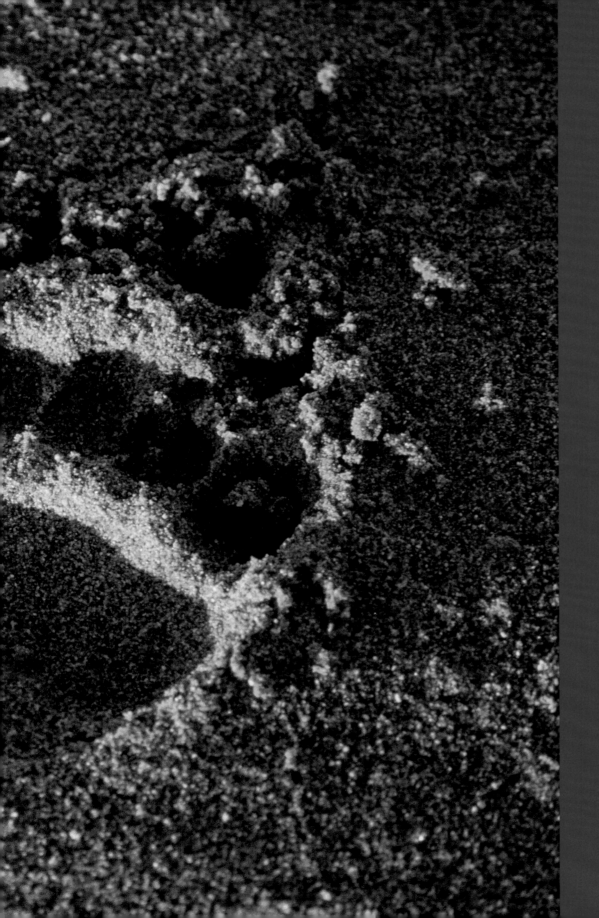

JOHN RALSTON SAUL

We must move away from the simplistic idea of human domination over place and towards a balance between people and place; a balance which says we are a new kind of high civilization which can imagine itself living in and with this land for as long as the trees grow, the sun rises from the east and sets in the west and the rivers flow.

At left: *Walking the beach of a taiga river.* James Raffan

Overleaf:
Early morning on the Berens River in northwestern Ontario during the summer of 2003. James Raffan

Stones of the Wind River

BRIAN BRETT

This is the land where all the rocks of the world are born,
  green or dusty desert pastel,
  galena and glitter,
  radioactive rocks,

crystals larger than the fist
  of the Gwich'in man
    who died here a thousand years ago.

This is where the earth gives birth
to the stones of the mountains,

  and they roll down,
  over the walls of fossils,

  down past the spruce taiga,
  screes and creek and rockfalls,

collecting in the river bed
all the stones of the world,

  shining beneath our red canoe —
  every colour and every form

  greater than human imagination.

And when we have blasted it,
mined it, polluted it, scavenged
the green hills to a desert and dust,
and when the sun finally flames out
in its last archangelic blast of energy
  this is where,
like elephants to their secret grotto,
all the rocks of the world will return.

Fritz Mueller

Fritz Mueller

My Prayer for the Boreal Forest

WILLIAM COMMANDA
Algonquin Elder

A William Commanda canoe, part of the collection of the Peterborough Canoe Museum, www.canoemuseum.net.

We sit in front of the fire on this bitterly cold evening in January. We have tossed a white birchbark log into the fire.

I remember that night out there in the snow, seventy-five years ago. It was beautiful and white as I crossed the river. The night air was full of that dangerous, penetrating cold, the one that comes when Mother Earth invites you to breath deeply and enter the timeless sleep of the happy hunting grounds. I forced myself to keep trudging to the forest at the edge of the shores of the river. There, I found the pile of collected dead wood standing up, towering over the snowdrifts, as my father had placed it a season ago when he taught me how to anticipate the needs of future travellers.

I lit my fire, and my mind strayed to the four big timberwolves who had found me here on their territory a year earlier, when I was fourteen. I remember so clearly how frightened my little dog was, how I had to hold him tight to quieten him. After a long time, the leader of the wolf pack sniffed loudly into the night sky, lay on the snow on his back and wiggled around, then leapt up and howled as he bounded off into the trees.

We were all one, then. The great mother, our great mother, threw her mantle of protection and provision over us all as she taught us to grow strong and brave and resilient, and respectful of the four elements upon which all life depends. That is how we understood what mother meant. And our great father: I saw him up there in night sky, with countless stars, including my special star, Ojigkwanong, after which I was named. He comforted me with the knowledge that I was not alone there at the forest's edge. As our rivers connected us Mamuwinini, us nomads, from one sacred island of fire to another, across the great rivers and lakes of Turtle Island, so we were also intimately connected to a greater reality.

But, not understanding the dangers inherent in translating and communicating concepts, we trusted other great mothers and fathers and gradually our own relationship with Mother Earth was eroded. We failed her in our task as caretakers.

I worry now that the loss is almost irrevocable. I watch this burning birchbark log and I weep because I know that I can no longer find birchbark large enough to build one of those canoes with which my ancestors traversed their world. And as we cut the trees, we erode the soil, and Mother Earth cannot hold the rains, and we suffer floods, and the air fills with contaminants.

But spirit is also strong and regenerative. I see the prayers of the new people in my homeland join with mine and aim the arrow of awareness into the masses. In this way, we give voice to the wild things and the wild places and reestablish the lines of allegiance with Mother Earth.

May the winds blow fresh across the boreal forest and drive new life into its heart. Megwetch, Mishomis, that I am a part of this prayer.

Ancient pictographs of canoe, Misshepezhieu (the great lynx), and mythical serpents at Agawa Rock on Lake Superior speak of abiding relationships between people and place. James Raffan

Contributors

ELAINE ALEXIE was raised in Fort McPherson and is a member of the Tetlit Gwich'in First Nation. She is a busy advocate for her people and for the land. In 2001, Elaine earned the Northern Conservation Award for her work to protect the Arctic Refuge. In August 2002, she was a youth delegate to the United Nations World Summit on Sustainable Development in Johannesburg, South Africa. And, in 2003, she was an active participant in Boreal Rendezvous, taking part in the Wind River journey and speaking at the closing ceremony in Ottawa. Elaine is currently the community outreach representative for CPAWS Yukon.

LAUREL ARCHER is a respected wilderness adventurer, guide, outdoor educator and patron of the CPAWS Boreal Program. She's been guiding canoe trips in northern Saskatchewan for 15 years, and has canoed and kayaked rivers all over the globe. Her writing has been published in numerous magazines and in a new book, *Northern Saskatchewan Canoe Trips: A Guide to 15 Wilderness Rivers*. Laurel was a guide for Rendezvous trips on the Churchill and Dease Rivers.

ANNA BAGGIO is the director of Northern Boreal Program for CPAWS–Wildlands League. As a biologist, she has studied spotted turtles and other reptiles and amphibians of Georgian Bay Islands National Park, as well as the design and implementation of ecologically sustainable agricultural practices in southern Costa Rica. Currently she sits on the Protected Areas Working Group of the Northern Boreal Initiative. Anna co-led the Berens River Rendezvous trip.

LINDA ANNE BAKER is a psychologist and photographer who is passionate about photographing birds, flowers, water and landscapes, particularly in abstract and "painterly" styles. A member of the Canadian Association for Photographic Art, she has published her images in magazines such as *Photo Life, Canadian Camera, Islands, Seasons, Lake Superior, WildBird*, and *Birds of the Wild*, as well as in the book *Birds of the Kingston Region*.

MARTEN BERKMAN was born in Montreal, studied visual arts and geography, and has explored landscapes around the world with his camera. His work appears in several books and magazines, including *Yukon Wild, Up Here* and *Canadian Geographic*. His fine-art landscape photography has been featured in several solo and group exhibits, and published as a limited-edition tritone book, *Chasms of Silence*. Marten lives with his wife, Jennifer, and daughter, Sya, upstream from Whitehorse, Yukon, and was part of Rendezvous' Snake River crew.

RON BOLT is a musician and artist whose paintings of the Canadian landscape and rugged coastlines place him firmly in the Northern Romantic tradition. Elected to the Royal Canadian Academy of Arts in 1985, his work has been shown at over 60 one-man exhibitions in Canadian galleries from St. John's, Newfoundland to Vancouver, British Columbia. Ron was a participant in the Snake River Rendezvous trip.

BRIAN BRETT is a Salt Spring Island poet, journalist and fiction writer. A former publisher at the Governor-General's award-winning literary press Blackfish, Brian is the author of ten books of fiction and poetry, and has appeared in numerous anthologies. His most recent book, *Uproar's Your Only Music — a memoir / selected poems*, was published this spring. Brian was a participant in the Wind River trip.

PETER BREWSTER is the newly retired night managing editor of the *Toronto Sun*. He began canoeing in 1967 after immigrating to Canada from England. He is a charter member of the Hide-Away Canoe Club and has participated in many ambitious canoe expeditions in the last 20 years. Peter lives in Toronto with his partner, Christie Campbell, and their daughter, Alison.

GERALD BUTTS is the Deputy Principal Secretary to the Premier of Ontario, Dalton McGuinty. Gerald developed his love for the outdoors through his childhood on Cape Breton Island. He and his wife, Jodi, have canoed, kayaked, hiked and camped through many of North America's National Parks and protected areas. They live in the High Park area of Toronto. Gerald was invited to join the Boreal Rendezvous expedition on the Nahanni River to paddle with his friend Justin Trudeau.

ANDREW CHAPESKI is a musician, lawyer, economic development specialist, facilitator, and principal of the Taiga Institute for Land, Culture and Economy based in Kenora, Ontario. He is a long-time land-use planning consultant to the Pikangikum First Nation and was instrumental in negotiations that led to the cooperation agreement that is featured in this book. Andrew met the Berens River crew on the beach at Pikangikum and along with translator Randolph Suggashie helped orchestrate the inclusion of elders' comments in *Rendezvous with the Wild*.

CHRISMAR MAPPING SERVICES (Mark Smith and Christine Kennedy) is one of Canada's premier makers of fine custom maps and purveyors of cartographic services. Based in Uxbridge, Ontario, this couple's city guides have helped people navigate some of the world's most complex urban jungles and their adventure maps have helped wilderness aficionados travel to the ends of the Earth.

WILLIAM COMMANDA is a respected Algonquin elder from Maniwaki, a long-time bark canoe builder, and honorary elder of the CPAWS Boreal Program. The elder's symbolic connection to the spiritual heritage of his people is reflected in his acclaimed, uniquely stenciled birchbark canoes, as well as in his tireless work to unite people of different backgrounds to the causes of peace and environmental stewardship. William Commanda participated in both the ceremonial launch, in Toronto, and the ceremonial conclusion of Boreal Rendezvous, on the shores of the Ottawa River, at the Museum of Civilization in Hull.

GWEN CURRY, from Brentwood, British Columbia, is an installation artist whose work explores the environment as subject matter, with a special focus on flora and fauna, both living and extinct. She was one of the artists selected to participate in the Three Rivers initiative in the Yukon and joined the Rendezvous team on the Bonnet Plume River trip.

WADE DAVIS is a scientist, author, photographer, speaker, and patron of the CPAWS Boreal Program. He is explorer-in-residence at the National Geographic Society and holds degrees from Harvard University in Anthropology, Biology and Ethnobotany. He has published over a hundred scientific and popular works on subjects ranging from Haitian vodoun to global biodiversity. His book *One River* was nominated for a Governor General's Award. His most recent book is *Light at the Edge of the World* (2002).

BRIAN DEINES is an artist and illustrator acclaimed for the warmth of his palette and his ability to breathe life into his images. He is a graduate of the Alberta College of Art. His illustrations bring to life the stories in several popular children's books, including *Sky Sisters* and *Bear on the Train*, published by Kids Can Press. *Dragon Fly Kites* (2002), written by Tomson Highway, was shortlisted for the Governor General's Award and nominated for the Schwartz Children's Literature Award. Brian was a participant in the Rendezvous journey on the Churchill River.

DAVID DODGE, first executive director of the Edmonton chapter of CPAWS, is a respected photographer and environmental journalist and was the founding editor of *Borealis* magazine. His radio work includes the award-winning 300-episode EcoFile radio series on sustainability and recently the Climate Change Show, a 23-week series focusing on climate change, at the CKUA Radio Network. Currently David is working with the Pembina Institute on Greenlearning.ca, an innovative online environmental education project. David participated in the Boreal Rendezvous as the photographer for the Athabasca River journey and the local Edmonton celebration.

KEN DRYDEN is an acclaimed sports personality and author. The winner of six Stanley Cups with the Montreal Canadiens, six-time all-star, recipient of five Vezina Trophies as the NHL's top goaltender and a member of the Hockey Hall of Fame, Dryden left his job as vice-chairman of Maple Leaf Sports and Entertainment in 2004 to run successfully as a federal Liberal Member of Parliament. He has written four best-selling books. *The Game* was named one of Canada's 100 most important books of the 20th century. His other titles are *Home Game*, *The Moved and the Shaken*, and *In School*. He has also served as Youth Commissioner for Ontario. Ken was a participant on the Rendezvous trip on the Athabasca River.

TERESA EARLE is a Whitehorse-based freelance writer whose recent credits include *The Globe and Mail*, *Up Here* magazine and *Alternatives Journal*. She also writes a weekly science and nature column in *The Yukon News*, in addition to writing and consulting for clients in tourism, business, human resources, conservation and information technology. With her partner, photographer Fritz Mueller, Teresa participated in the Wind River journey.

MALCOLM EDWARDS is a paddling enthusiast and conservation volunteer living in the Ottawa area. Malcolm's great affinity for the outdoors has led him to canoe and kayak extensively across Canada. He was involved in all aspects of the Boreal Rendezvous project right from the beginning, ensuring that it became more than just a great idea on paper. Malcolm participated in and helped to guide the Dease River journey.

WENDY FRANCIS is the Toronto-based chairperson of the Yellowstone to Yukon Conservation Initiative. Educated in biology and environmental law, her professional experience includes five years of law practice, training senior government managers in public consultation techniques, teaching environmental law, ENGO organizational development and capacity building, and senior conservation campaign design and delivery. Wendy is married to Harvey Locke, and together they participated in the Rendezvous journey on the Nahanni River.

TIM GRAY was executive director of the CPAWS–Wildlands League from 1990 to 2003, during which time he was co-chair of the Forest for Tomorrow Coalition in the Provincial Timber Class Environmental Assessment hearing, as well as a member of the Old Growth Forest Policy Advisory Committee and Ontario coordinator of the World Wildlife Fund's Endangered Spaces campaign. In 2003, Tim participated in the Moisie River trip and became CPAWS director of Boreal Forest Programs.

WILLIAM T. GRIFFIN was born near Stanley, New Brunswick, in 1881 and spent much of his life in business with his father, catering to and guiding sportsmen from New Brunswick and New England. Even as a proud great-grandfather, before his death in 1974, Bill Griffin retained a lively interest in the world around him, including the drafting of an autobiographical book of prose and poetry called *You're on the Miramichi*, published posthumously in 1981.

SARAH HARMER is a singer and songwriter known for her honest approach and sensitive style. She grew up in southern Ontario, where she formed the band Weeping Tile. She has also played with the Indigo Girls, Moxy Fruvous and Great Big Sea and has collaborated with groups such as the Tragically Hip. Since 1999, Sarah has produced two critically-acclaimed solo albums, *Songs for Clem* and *You Were Here*, which went gold in Canada in 2001. Sarah was one of the music-speaking participants in the Rendezvous trip on the Moisie River.

NEIL HARTLING is an outfitter, guide and author who fell in love with the South Nahanni River more than 30 years ago. Reading of the grand river with the beautiful name, he was fascinated by the legends of the canyons and the promise of adventure. The allure proved irresistible. He has spent the last 20 years living out these dreams, writing two books, *Nahanni, River of Gold/River of Dreams* and *Alaska to Nunavut, the Great River*. Neil makes his home in Whitehorse, Yukon, and was guide on Rendezvous' Nahanni River trip.

TOMSON HIGHWAY is an author and musician as well as one of Canada's leading playwrights and a patron of the CPAWS Boreal Program. He has written eight plays and has received both the Dora Mavor Moore Award and the Chalmers Award. His first novel, *Kiss of the Fur Queen*, appeared in 1998, and his latest children's book, *Dragonfly Kites*, written in Cree and English, was released in 2002. A member of the Order of Canada and a recipient of an Aboriginal Achievement Award, he is the former artistic director of Native Earth Performing Arts Inc., Toronto's only professional Native theatre company.

BRUCE HILL is the CPAWS campaigner for northern British Columbia and has been involved over the years in the efforts to protect the Kitlope Watershed and to reform federal fisheries policy on the North Coast of BC. He has an eclectic background, from civil rights activist in the 1960s to sawyer and sawmill operator; mechanic to fishing guide and eco-tourism operator. If he's not on the job, you'll find him in a boat somewhere off the coast, or on a wilderness river fishing for steelhead. Bruce took part in the Dease River trip.

OLIVER HILL is a member and band councillor of the Pikangikum First Nation and participated in the cooperation agreement signing ceremony on the shores of the Berens River that was part of Boreal Rendezvous in the summer of 2003.

HELEN HOY is professor of English and Women's Studies at the University of Guelph, having previously taught at the universities of Toronto, Manitoba, Lethbridge, and Minnesota. She has published *Modern English-Canadian Prose* and *How Should I Read These? Native Women Writers in Canada*, and co-edited with Thomas King and Cheryl Calver, *The Native in Literature*. With her spouse, Thomas King, and son, Ben, Helen participated in the Churchill River expedition.

ANNE JANSSEN is CPAWS National Boreal Coordinator and was one of the moving forces behind the scenes who ensured the ultimate success of Boreal Rendezvous. She has "officially" been advocating for the environment since 1990 when she joined Greenpeace as a canvasser. From 1995 to 1998, Anne was international coordinator of the Taiga Rescue Network, based in Sweden. Anne was a member of the Churchill River team.

CATHY JONES is a patron of the CPAWS Boreal Program, a Gemini award-winning actor and writer, and a founding member of the hit comedy troupe CODCO. She is Canada's leading lady of character-driven comedy and has starred in the hit CBC series *This Hour Has 22 Minutes* since it began in 1993. She is currently touring her new stage show, *Me, Dad and the Hundred Boyfriends*, and is shooting her feature documentary, *The Dogs Who Ate My Homework*. Cathy was a participant on the Berens River journey and hosted the Rendezvous final celebrations in Ottawa in September 2003.

THOMAS KING is a writer and popular CBC radio personality who teaches Native literature and creative writing at the University of Guelph. He created and performed in the CBC radio show *The Dead Dog Café Comedy Hour*. His books include the novels *Green Grass, Running Water*, *Truth and Bright Water* and *Medicine River*, as well as a collection of short stories and two children's books. Of Cherokee origin, he was born in California and moved to Canada in 1980. He was a participant on the Churchill and Coal River trips.

PATRICK LANE is considered by many writers and critics to be the finest poet of his generation. He has published 25 books of poetry and prose in the past 40 years and has edited several significant anthologies of poetry and nonfiction. He presently resides in Victoria, BC.

DAVID LANG is president of the CPAWS–Wildlands League and has served on the board of the Wildland League since 1991. He is a former cattle breeder and teacher. At present he is taking time to reflect on the state of the planet, to travel with his wife, Sally, and to help with the careers of their three children. Dave joined the Rendezvous crew on the Berens River.

MELODY LEPINE describes herself as a "grassroots Cree and Dene woman" who is the Environmental Affairs Coordinator with the Mikisew Cree First Nation Industry Relations Corporation (IRC) in Fort McMurray, Alberta. A graduate in Environmental Conservation Sciences from University of Alberta, she works to maintain the cultural integrity of the Mikisew Cree First Nation and the ecological integrity of their lands, as well as to educate Canadians about the importance of our boreal forest and the true fabric that binds it all together. Melody was a participant on the Athabasca River leg of Boreal Rendezvous.

HARVEY LOCKE is a native of Calgary who is currently a senior program advisor to Tides Canada Foundation based in Toronto. He is also VP, Conservation, of the Canadian Parks and Wilderness Society, a board member of the Y to Y Conservation Initiative, a director emeritus of the Wildlands Project, and a member of the World Commission on Protected Areas. In 1999, *Time Canada* magazine named him one of Canada's leaders for the 21st century. Harvey and his wife, Wendy Francis, were participants on Rendezvous' Nahanni River expedition.

GWENDOLYN MacEWEN was one of Canada's finest 20th-century poets. Her collection *The Shadow Maker* won the Governor General's Award for poetry in 1969. Born in 1941, her first published poem appeared in *The Canadian Forum* when she was seventeen. She left school at eighteen to concentrate on her writing and, until she died in 1987, produced a substantial body of work, samples of which are included in most Canadian anthologies.

ANDREA MAENZA has been involved with the CPAWS–Wildlands League in one capacity or another since 1996. She has volunteered as a photographer, and on trail cleanups and forest audits. She was also the local coordinator of the Goulais River Watershed Project, linking wilderness protection with community economic development. She is currently on the board of the Wildlands League and continues to photograph for them and advocate passionately for wilderness protection from her home in Courtice, Ontario. Andrea laughed her way down the Berens River in the summer of 2003 with her Rendezvous compatriots.

JOYCE MAJISKI is a biologist and self-taught artist who draws on the strength of her connection to the natural world as the basis of her creative energy. Originally from Sudbury, Ontario, she graduated from the University of Guelph in 1981 before moving north to work as a waterfowl field specialist. She started guiding in 1988, leading hiking trips in Kluane, and moving into whitewater rafting in the early '90s. Joyce is co-owner of Sila Sojourns and lives in a log cabin just outside Whitehorse. She joined Rendezvous as an artist on the Wind River trip.

JOSÉ MANSILLA-MIRANDA is a visual artist who strives to reconnect his psychological and symbolic memory with the ancestral memory of the Americas. His constant goal is to awaken and expand his consciousness in harmony with nature, through exploration of his artistic creativity and cultural identity. As one of the selected artists on the Three Rivers Project and a participant on the Rendezvous trip on the Snake River, he used the process of his art to connect with the northern landscape and the fragile environment.

REBECCA MASON is an artist, canoeing instructor and patron of the CPAWS Boreal Program. Based in Chelsea, Québec, she acquired her paddling skills and her fondness for canoes from her father, Bill Mason. Her artwork has been displayed in a wide array of exhibitions and galleries in Ontario and Québec. Becky has contributed to several canoeing books, produced an award-winning video entitled *Classic Solo Canoeing*, and speaks frequently about her love of the wild. Becky and her husband, Reid McLachlan, were participants on the Berens River trip.

CARRIE McGOWN is an Outdoor Recreation and Geography graduate from Lakehead University, an experienced canoeist, and half of the human spirit behind "Many Waters," a three-summer cross-country canoe journey (1999–2001) to raise awareness about the value of Canada's wilderness heritage.

REID McLACHLAN is a visual artist, canoeist and canoe builder. He works in his studio in Gatineau Hills from October to May, occasionally taking time to ski and tend to his rink on the river. The summer is spent building and repairing canoes and, whenever possible, escaping on wilderness river canoe trips with his wife, Becky Mason. Reid was a participant on the Berens River segment of Boreal Rendezvous.

LACHLIN McKINNON is a musician, lawyer and special advisor to the Governor General. As a canoeist and photographer, he was one of those who accompanied His Excellency John Ralston Saul down the Snake River in the summer of 2003.

COURTNEY MILNE is a freelance photographer who concentrates on landscape and nature imagery. He has written articles, produced books, conducted workshops, seminars, worldwide photographic tours, and presented more than 200 public performances of his multimedia shows. He's travelled to 35 countries, on all seven continents, taking photographs for a series of books called *The Sacred Earth Collection*. Courtney took part in the Bonnet Plume segment of the Three Rivers portion of Boreal Rendezvous.

MARCEL MORIN is a cartographer and a GIS specialist employed by Timberline Forest Inventory Consultants in Vancouver, British Columbia. For the past six years, he has worked with Whitefeather Forest Management Corporation and the Taiga Institute, developing Indigenous Knowledge mapping templates used by the community research teams. He visits the Pikangikum First Nation yearly to facilitate training of the research team in GIS mapping technology.

MARTHA MORTSON is a graduate of the Outdoor Recreation, Parks and Tourism program at Lakehead University and was the leader and half of the human spirit behind "Many Waters," a three-summer (1999–2001) canoe journey from St. John, NB, to Tuktoyaktuk, NT.

FRITZ MUELLER is a wildlife biologist and nature photographer based in Whitehorse. For a decade he has worked on biology and environmental assessment issues in the Yukon and Northwest Territories. His photographs have been widely published and in 2003 won the Banff Mountain Photography Grand Prize as well the top prize in the competition's landscape category. With his spouse, Teresa Earle, Fritz paddled the Wind River with Boreal Rendezvous.

MICHAEL and GEOFFREY PEAKE are two of the four paddling Peake brothers who make up half of the Hide-Away Canoe Club. Michael is a Toronto-based journalist and Geoff is a teacher in Nelson, BC. Michael also publishes the canoeing journal *Che-Mun*. The HACC specializes in historically based trips and in 1985 named a river in Nunavut after Eric Morse.

CHARLIE PETERS is former Chief of the Pikangikum First Nation. He was one of the elders who rose to speak at the signing ceremony in Pikangikum that was part of the Berens River segment of Boreal Rendezvous.

GIDEON PETERS is a trapper and elder and one of the members of the Pikangikum First Nation who took part as a guide and interpreter for the Boreal Rendezvous crew in a day-long excursion to historic and culturally significant sites along the Berens River.

PADDY PETERS is Chief of the Pikangikum First Nation and was the host and master of ceremonies for the community feast on the shores of the Berens River at which the Partnership Framework Agreement between the people of Pikangikum and the Partnership for Public Lands was signed.

NORMAN QUILL is a member of the Pikangikum First Nation and an elder who played an integral role during Boreal Rendezvous, in helping participants on the Berens River expedition understand the deep cultural significance of wild rice and other medicinal plants of the boreal.

JIMMY RANKIN is a critically acclaimed singer and songwriter who, after numerous hits and multiple Juno awards with Canadian musical family the Rankins, made his solo debut with the CD *Song Dog*. Although often slotted in the country category, his style and music have a broad appeal and have garnered numerous awards. With his wife, Mia, Jimmy participated in Rendezvous' Dease River trip.

JOHN RALSTON SAUL is an award-winning essayist and novelist as well as the honorary patron of the CPAWS Boreal Program. He is the author of *On Equilibrium* and *Reflections of a Siamese Twin*, in which he presents ideas on the nature of Canada. This book was chosen by *Maclean's* as one of the ten best nonfiction books of the 20th century. His passion for nature, water and Canadian history meet in the quintessential Canadian mode of transportation— the canoe. He joined Boreal Rendezvous during trips on the Snake and Ottawa Rivers.

CANDACE SAVAGE is an author who shares in her work both a love for language and for the natural world around her. She graduated as gold medallist from the University of Alberta and now lives and writes in Saskatoon. She is the author of 21 books of nonfiction, most of which focus on wildlife or cultural history, including books on birds and animals or western Canada. Her most recent book, *Wizards: An Amazing Journey Through the Last Great Age of Magic*, was honoured by the Canadian Science Writers Association and the Saskatchewan Book Awards. Candace was a participant in Rendezvous' Churchill River expedition.

DAVID SCHINDLER is Killam Memorial Professor of Ecology at the University of Alberta. He founded and directed the Experimental Lakes Project of the Canadian Department of Fisheries and Oceans, conducting interdisciplinary research on the effects of climate change on boreal ecosystems. His work has been used globally in the formulation of ecologically sound management policies. Dr. Schindler has received numerous research awards, including Canada's highest scientific honor, the NSERC Gerhard Herzberg Gold Medal for Science and Engineering, in 2001. David Schindler was a participant on Rendezvous' Athabasca River journey.

MARTA SCYTHES is an artist and biologist who has established a solid reputation for her work in pencil, pen, etching and watercolour. *Harrowsmith* magazine, Telemedia Publishing, McClelland & Stewart, and HarperCollins USA have published books containing her illustrations, including McClelland & Stewart's *Up North* series and *The Canadian Encyclopedia*.

GEORGE SMITH is the National Conservation Director for CPAWS. He sits on the Muskwa–Kechika Advisory Board, Tetrahedron Park Advisory Committee, and the Environment Committee of the Vancouver Foundation. In 1997, he was co-recipient of the first achievement award given by the Yellowstone to Yukon Conservation Initiative. George and his partner, Merrily Corder, live in Gibsons, BC. He joined Rendezvous's Coal River trip.

DONALD STANDFIELD is a photographer who was introduced to wilderness canoeing at an early age and spent much of his childhood on field assignments with his father, a noted Canadian biologist. He is co-author, with Liz Lundell, of *Algonquin: The Park and Its People* and *Stories from the Bow Seat*, the latter of which was the design inspiration for *Rendezvous with the Wild*. Don lives in Toronto with his spouse, Linda Leckie, and still tries to spend as much time as possible in Algonquin Park.

HUGH STEWART has been a devout wilderness paddler for many decades. In the 1970s and 1980s, he ran a wilderness travel business in Temagami, where he was a pioneer in the effort to create the Lady Evelyn–Smoothwater Wilderness Park. In recent years, Hugh has become a forest technician and a woodlot owner. His home and canoe shop are in the Gatineau Hills, north of Ottawa.

GEORGE B. STRANG is an elder of the Pikangikum First Nation and was one of the community members who served as guides, instructors and hosts for a day on the land for the Boreal Rendezvous Berens River crew. George is one a number of elders who spoke passionately of the need for cooperation and sharing in ensuring the long-term health of the boreal forest and all of the people and animals it sustains.

DAVID SUZUKI is an award-winning scientist, environmentalist, broadcaster, and a world leader in sustainable ecology. He is well known as the chair of the David Suzuki Foundation and host of CBC's popular science program *The Nature of Things*. He is professor emeritus with UBC's Sustainable Development Research Institute and has received numerous awards for his work, including the Order of Canada and formal adoption by two First Nations tribes. David helped launch Boreal Rendezvous in Toronto and took part in the Athabasca River portion of the project.

IAN TAMBLYN is a musician, adventurer, playwright, and one of Canada's premier folk artists. Known for his lyrical interpretations of back country experiences in folk songs, soundtracks and audioscapes, Ian has won several Canadian music awards and has just completed his 24th recording project. Although he is headed into DVD production with the new creative possibilities for combining sound and imagery offered by emerging microcomputer technology, his writing and artistic sensibilities remain rooted in the natural environment.

JUSTIN TRUDEAU is the chair of the Katimavik board of directors, where he works to increase the skills and engagement of Canada's youth in their country, their communities and their environment. He is also a director of the Canadian Avalanche Foundation, where he promotes intelligent risk-taking and awareness regarding wilderness safety and back-country adventuring. He has worked as a camp counsellor in Algonquin Park, a whitewater river guide on the Rouge River, a snowboard instructor at Whistler–Blackcomb, and a high-school teacher in Vancouver. He is presently studying mechanical engineering at l'Ecole Polytechnique de l'Universite de Montréal. Justin joined Rendezvous on the Nahanni River.

SUZA' TSETSO is a spiritual and cultural interpreter-facilitator for Spirit Discoveries in Fort Simpson, Northwest Territories. She is a member of the Deh Cho First Nation and carries with her a depth of knowledge about the cultural significance of the Nahanni River. Suza' has strong family ties to the land, enjoys interacting with elders and youth, and, with her excellent sense of humour, is an excellent storyteller. She was part of the Rendezvous team on the Nahanni River.

SOLOMON TURTLE is a member of the Pikangikum First Nation and one of the elders who spoke at length at the Berens River signing feast and celebration about the value of cooperation and collaboration in the future management and sustainable development of the boreal forest.

ROMOLA VASANTHA is a retired public servant who worked primarily in the federal justice system in corrections, policing, and Aboriginal and restorative justice across Canada. Born in South Africa, she studied English Literature at McMaster University, and now works around the clock to support the efforts of Elder William Commanda through the Circle of All Nations, a global eco-community dedicated to indigenous wisdom and environmental issues, social justice, racial harmony and peace-building.

BRIGITTE VOSS is a geographer and biologist with three years' professional experience working with the Canadian Parks and Wilderness Society (CPAWS) in Québec. She was instrumental in the establishment of the Montréal chapter and its first executive director. Brigitte was responsible for organizing the Moisie River expedition of Boreal Rendezvous.

ROBERTA WALKER is a writer, photographer and broadcaster whose work on nature and environment has appeared in numerous publications, including *Canadian Geographic, Reader's Digest, Chatelaine,* and *The Globe and Mail,* and on CBC Radio. She has canoed, hiked and explored many parts of Canada's boreal, from east to west, and was part of the Boreal Rendezvous organizing team in 2003.

CATHY WILKINSON is the director and cofounder of the Canadian Boreal Initiative. She played a key role in bringing together leading conservation organizations, resource companies and First Nations to create the Boreal Forest Conservation Framework, which, after release on December 1, 2003, was called the "most extensive national conservation vision ever." Cathy was one of 17 Canadians who participated in Rendezvous' Athabasca River journey.

GREG YEOMAN is Conservation Director for CPAWS–NWT and an original member of both the NWT Protected Areas Strategy Implementation Advisory Committee and the Sahyoue/Edacho Candidate Protected Area Working Group. Prior to this, after completing his masters in Environmental Science at York University, he was coordinator of the South Country Protected Areas Project, a grassroots conservation initiative to protect remaining natural areas in the prairie and parklands of southern Alberta. Greg was part of Rendezvous' Nahanni River trip.

Permissions

"Dark Pines Under Water," by Gwendolyn MacEwen, reprinted by permission of her sister and executor, Carol Wilson.

"A Sunset in New Brunswick," reprinted by permission of the Central New Brunswick Woodsmen's Museum and William T. Griffin's grandson.

"The Carpenter," reprinted by permission of Patrick Lane.

If you'd like to learn more about CPAWS and its boreal program, contact:
info@cpaws.org or 1-800-333-WILD (9453)

CPAWS National Office
c/o Boreal Program
880 Wellington Street, Suite 506
Ottawa, Ontario
K1R 6K7
www.cpaws.org/boreal

FSC is the only certification standard recognized by CPAWS as requiring environmentally, economically and socially responsible forest management. Forests certified to meet this standard will help us achieve our vision of conserving Canada's boreal forest by protecting wild areas and changing forestry practices. CPAWS chapters have contributed greatly to the development of the FSC boreal forest standard and are now promoting its adoption by companies across the country. Using FSC-certified Domtar Luna, gloss, 100 lb. text, this is the first hardcover book printed in Canada to carry the FSC label. (20% certified virgin wood fiber, SW-COC-880)

The FSC Trademark identifies products that contain wood from well-managed forests certified in accordance with the rules of the Forest Stewardship Council.

Printed in Canada by Friesens (FSC Certified SW-COC-1271)

FSC

20% minimum   FSC Trademark © 1996 Forest Stewardship Council A.C.

In November 2004, the Canadian Parks and Wilderness Society (CPAWS) will launch *Rendezvous With the Wild* as part of its national **True North Wild and Free** celebration of Canada's boreal forest. The ten-city tour will be hosted by the book's editor, James Raffan, and feature as special guests, many of the contributors to this book.

We would like to thank our partners and supporters in this initiative

as well as our partners in and sponsors of Boreal Rendezvous 2003,
without whom this project would not have happened

for their support and assistance in the production of this book

Acknowledgments

Like Boreal Rendezvous, the 10-river summer caper in which the book has its genesis, Rendezvous with the Wild is a work of many hearts and willing hands.

To the organizers of those ten sovereign river trips through the boreal in the summer of 2003 — to our guides, outfitters, travel agents, and sponsors; to the community members and forest industry people who helped along the way; and to the volunteers who so ably convened countless associated Rendezvous events, I say thank you, and well done.

The dream of this project was to create a volume that would celebrate the boreal and reflect the diversity of enthusiasms held by all of those who took part in Boreal Rendezvous. With wonderful raw material, support from CPAWS staffers and sponsors across the country, and with the expertise of the hard-working Boston Mills crew, that dream has become real. There are a thousand reasons in this book to care about the boreal. It was made to be shared.

To the seventy-plus contributors who submitted songs, stories, artwork, and photos to create this handsome book — all of whom have work in here somewhere — to Anne Janssen at CPAWS national office, publisher John Denison, managing editor Noel Hudson, designer Gillian Stead and especially to all our family members who made it possible for these labours to happen, I say merci beaucoup. Together, we did it!

Now, with this book as a reminder of how inspiring is the boreal and what can result when we collaborate, let us be similarly creative and diligent in ensuring a sustainable future for the boreal. That remains a worthy work in progress.

James Raffan, editor
Seeley's Bay, Ontario
July 2004

The nineteenth hole, Thelon Boreal Links, Thelon River, NWT. James Raffan